Stories and Sermons of Survival:

Meeting God in the Wilderness

Carl D. Tuyl

PublishAmerica
Baltimore

First printing

At the specific preference of the author, PublishAmerica allowed this work to remain exactly as the author intended, verbatim, without editorial input.

ISBN: 1-4241-2721-1
PUBLISHED BY PUBLISHAMERICA, LLLP
www.publishamerica.com
Baltimore

Printed in the United States of America

To Martha Who Awaited My Return For Seven Years Of War

Acknowledgements

Dr. Mary Kooy was an ever present source of inspiration and encouragement. Corrie my daughter patiently guided me through all those stages of completing the manuscript.

CHAPTER ONE
HUNGRY FOOD FANTASIES

Waffles! Great big heaping mountains of golden brown waffles with syrup dripping from them. Whipped cream piled on top of them like snow on the Rocky Mountains. That would be the dessert. I had a bit of trouble making that decision for there were so many alternatives to consider. What about a whole apple pie? Heated and with brown sugar on top. Or one of those gigantic mocha cakes my mother used to bake. I had thought about that and ranked it among the possibilities.

Like every other night I had great difficulty determining the dinner menu. So many options! Pork chops with sauerkraut and thick smoked sausages. Or just pea soup with a piece of smoked ham settled at the bottom of the pan like gold waiting to be mined. I had finally settled on balls of delicately spiced and fried lean hamburger with a mustard sauce, cauliflower and tiny boiled potatoes The smell of food came powerfully into my senses like music from speakers turned too loud.

The choice of beverage was easy. No hour-long deliberation on that score. Simply a keg of Heineken. One of those old fashioned wooden barrels. Men who wore corduroy suits with leather patches on their shoulders used to deliver them in my hometown. They screwed the tap into the barrel and drew a glass to check the quality of the beer. I had seen them do it at the family gatherings when all my aunts and uncles celebrated some occasion.

It took a while to get everything prepared. I followed the instructions of the cookbook to the letter, making only slight creative adjustments with the spices. I had invited some people and we were about to start when....

"Heraus du Schweinhund, aus, aus, aus." The German S.S. guard walked past the bunks screaming and swearing his gutteral curses, hitting prisoners with his stick. All of a sudden the place was full of the noise of awaking people. It was still dark. I wondered what had happened. That cruel waking call usually happened at six o'clock in the morning when the first light of the day hesitantly stole through the small windows. It was always accompanied by the clanging of a bell. The bell did not sound this time. This was no ordinary morning parade. The angry excitement of the guard told me that something strange was about to happen.

I was prisoner 913 at the Amersfoort concentration camp in the Netherlands. I had been arrested during a night raid in the village where I was in hiding. At a very short and for me almost incomprehensible trial I had been condemned to twenty years of hard labour. I was only in the sixth month of my sentence, and my weight was already down to where my bones jutted through my skin. Hunger was a constant pain in my belly. All I could think of was food, and at night in my bunk I fantasized about these gourmet meals.

ACTS 16 : 16-34
"About midnight Paul and Silas were praying and singing hymns to God."

Paul and Silas, had obediently followed God's guidance. They were convinced that they had been called to bring the Gospel of Jesus Christ to Europe. They had set out immediately. No word of objection, no delay, no dilly-dallying. They set sail from Troas and via Samothrace they reached Neapolis, and set foot ashore. They headed immediately again for the city of Philippi where there was a large concentration of people. It had not been an easy journey, but already in Philippi they had seen the Spirit of God add the first convert of Europe to the church of Jesus Christ.

One would expect that both Paul and Silas would be rewarded in some fashion for their faithful obedience. Perhaps a public recognition of their heroic faith. Maybe a reception put on by the citizenry of Philippi. The keys to the city. Flowers given to them by little girls, and a dinner with the leading authorities.

Instead they get thrown into the clink. Way down in solitary confinement, their feet tied to the wall, their clothing torn and their backs bloodied by the lashes that had rained on them. That's how they wind up, lying half naked with bloodied backs on the stone cold floor of the dark dungeon.

I was in Philippi in the fall of 1975. I went down into that dungeon. I am pretty sure that it was the place where Paul and Silas had been imprisoned for there was no other multi-storied building in the ruins of the city. The small prison was still dark and damp, and it was as if the moans of the prisoners of the past still echoed between the walls. My own prison experience re-entered my mind like an unwanted visitor.

I sat down with my notebook on my knee and started to write this very sermon about Paul and Silas' songs in the night. There was much I did not understand. Why those two people in prison? "God," I said, "Something went wrong here. These were two important people for your church. They were the carriers of the Gospel. It was a very critical time. The very existence of the European church hung in the balance." And "God, didn't you choose those two men? So how come they landed in prison?"

Reading the passage there is the Peter-like temptation to correct God. To say: "You can't allow that. You have to encourage those two people. What if they lose heart here? What if they resign? What if they quit?"

Sometimes we argue with God that way." God, things are going awry. Things are going totally and absolutely haywire. God you got to do something." When we don't understand God's ways with us, we always think that things go wrong. And then we pour out our objections: "God you have to bring about change! This cannot go on any longer." Then our prayers become long and bitter complaints.

We would have expected that lament from Paul and Silas in that dark night in that Philippi prison hole: "God there has been a mistake. You are a hard God to serve." That complaint we would understand and expect.

But listen, from what inmates would call the hole, that very portal of hell, filled with suffering and misery, there comes the eerie sound of praises to God. And even though we do not get any explanation concerning this suffering, no answer to our "Why," we do hear the calming voice of God saying: "I give my people strength."

These Philippi songs of the night somehow become God's consolation for all believers. I give my people whatever strength they need in the circumstances of their lives."

No, there is no well-rounded theodicy for suffering in this passage. The backs of Paul and Silas bleed on the damp cold prison floor, and no explanation is offered. There is no sudden flash of insight that eases the agony. And yet there is light. The light of God's grace which is always sufficient and which always strengthens. The comfort of God's presence even in the darkest prison. It is that presence that enabled Paul and Silas to sing hymns of praise in that miserable night. God gives his people strength.

How is it possible to sing in the dark night of life? In the night of incurable illness, the night of old age, the night of suffering, the night of hopelessness, the night of depression, and the night of the cross, yes even in the night of death? All those anxious nights.

It is possible! It is possible to sing the songs of God's praise in the night. Yes it is, the text says, God's grace makes it possible. Call upon me in the day of trouble and you will experience my presence. my strength. The song in the night of life is the song of God's grace. I will never forsake you. I see that promise fulfilled in that dark Philippi prison hole. When the night comes God will enable you to sing songs of praise.

Hear again the words of the text: "About midnight Paul and Silas were praying and singing hymns to God." There is the temptation there to dwell on the courage of Paul and Silas. Sing our own hymns of praise about their strong faith, but they themselves would rise up and condemn us. If there is anything to boast, they would say boast in the cross of Jesus Christ. Sing of the grace of God. That comforting, encouraging, strengthening grace is visible in that Philippi prison of our Bible passage.

Another fear looms in that hole of a dungeon. With Paul and Silas in prison the Gospel is bound. This is a dead end for the spread of the gospel of Jesus Christ. The Gospel was on its way to Europe and it too winds up in that miserable prison. Another failure for how are they to believe in him of whom they have never heard? And how are they to hear without a preacher? The question of Romans 10. And see the preachers, like animals bound to the wall of the dungeon. This must be the end of the Gospel's march. Lydia will remain the sole and only convert.

The cause seems doomed to failure. Hang your head and quit hoping. This is the end. We know it. See the facts. How could there be a church in Europe? Look at the walls of that prison. Look at Paul and Silas beaten and bound. Look at the jailer armed to the teeth. The hope of a church in Europe shatters in thousand pieces on the rough floor of this prison, like a china cup under a bulldozer.

Look at that jailer. Sword on his side. He means business. He binds Paul and Silas to the wall. This is a victory for the devil, the bankruptcy of hope. Farewell to any prospect of progress for the Gospel. That jailer personifies the might of the night.

A smile must have gone through the heavens. That jailer? That armed guard? Is that what made you give up hope? Is it he who causes all your pessimism? Look, the Spirit of God is already winging its way to the man's heart. Who do you think will be the second convert in Europe? Who do you think is the next one to be born of the spirit?

Unbelief creeps into our minds. Him? Impossible! We are inclined to take the words of Ananias who was told to enlist Paul: "God you must be kidding." We throw up the facts as the vomit of our unbelief. Remember the two men who met Jesus on the way to Emmaus. "This is already the third day," they said in their hopelessness to him who had risen from the dead. The Israelites knew they would drown in the Red Sea, or by the Egyptian sword. And that Phillippian jailer too took our eyes away from God's powerful grace.

Well watch. An earthquake. The foundations of the prison shake, the doors open, the chains come loose and suddenly the armed-to-the-teeth jailer is dead scared.

In the twinkling of an eye the God of hope breaks through the might of the night. Listen to the jailer: "Men, what must I do to be saved?" Caught in our pessimism, in our inability to accept that God is the God of hope, we often give up too early. Those two disciples walking from Jerusalem to Emmaus said: "We had hoped but…" Yet they walked beside Him in whom God's power became visible for all ages: "He was crucified, died and was buried, he descended into hell, the third day he rose again from the dead."

In the nights of our doubts we see God's kingdom sabotaged and destroyed. We pointed at the prison, we looked at the jailer, and we saw no more hope. And there are the other dark hopeless nights: illness, adversity, widowhood, misery, the night of the cross. And we see in our Bible passage that God's way goes straight through the darkness. Who would not remember here that there was darkness from the sixth till the ninth hour on Golgotha.

God does new things (Isaiah 42:9). God is still today the God of hope. Exactly here hear from that dark dungeon, the great song of God's grace, the song of the gospel, the mighty song of Jesus Christ The song that echoes throughout the whole Bible: "Believe in the Lord Jesus and you will be saved." The night gives birth to the day, the darkness bore the great day of hope. His truth goes marching on.

The postscript, the end of the text: "He took them the same hour of the night, and washed their wounds, and he was baptized at once with all his family, then brought them up into the house, and he rejoiced with all his household that he had believed in God."

And here is a temptation: to look at Paul and Silas and say: "All is well that ends well." The night was too dark, and those words would be too cheap. Their backs still hurt. It is better to let God speak and not mix my words into that word of God. And this is his promise: in the end Paul and Silas I will wash your tears away, and death shall be no more, neither mourning, nor pain anymore for the former things shall have passed away.

CHAPTER TWO
BORN AGAIN IN A SMILE

The S.S. guard came back on my side of the barracks, hitting people indiscriminately. I was almost dressed. At my arrival at the camp my hair had been shaved and I was supplied with an old army uniform and wooden shoes. The guard passed my bunk cursing and yelling "Heraus, aus, aus." I hastened outside to the parade ground. I knew the place where I was supposed to be. Way back in the last row of my block.

Twice a day the camp population stood at parade to be counted. After the morning bell the day started with a quick washing at one of the cold water taps, making your bed, and getting your tea. Tea was a spoonful of hot water that had had only limited encounters with tealeaves. Soon after that we had to rush out for parade. We stood in rows of ten. Ten sideways, and ten behind each other. Blocks of one hundred prisoners.

S.S. soldiers inspected the sorry lot. Usually they found something wrong. A cap too lopsided, someone with fingers not exactly on the seam of the pants, or just someone whose looks they did not like. One of the guards would then yell "Nieder" which meant that the whole block had to throw themselves to the ground. Whether the ground was dry, or wet from rain did not make any difference. "Nieder," the guard would yell, and they would walk between the rows and hit anyone who in their opinion was not sufficiently "Nieder." After they had satisfied themselves that everyone was flat on the ground they yelled "Auf." Hardly on our legs again they would repeat the "Nieder."

13

"Nieder! Auf! Nieder! Auf!" Ever faster they would give their commands until they were ready to send the prisoners off to work.

There was something inexpressibly humiliating in this exercise. It sapped one's self esteem like water will slowly leak through a little crack at the bottom of a container. There were among the prisoners professors, justices, and many of Holland's prominent citizens, but upon the yelled command of a few uniformed nobodies we all had to grovel in the dirt.

The evening parade was even more severe. Groups of prisoners returned to the camp. When they passed the gate the guard yelled: *"Mutzen ab!"* The prisoners then passed the guardpost with their caps pressed to the seam of their pants, their bald heads turned to the officer at the gate. Inside the gate it was *"Mutzen auf,"* and quickly find your place in the parade formation.

The dead and the wounded were brought in on wheelbarrows. They were the victims of the S.S.'s wrath. Beaten to death, or maimed into paralysis by continued and crushing torture. Especially Jewish prisoners were often singled out for death inflicting cruelties. Neither death nor inability to stand were deemed an excuse for evening parade. The prisoners had to be counted, and the numbers had to show that nobody had escaped during the day.

Evening parade was also the time that the punishments were meted out for infractions of the rules that had taken place during the day. A lot of *"Auf"* and *"Nieder,"* but also cruel and often deadly beatings in front of the assembled camp population.

A favourite S.S. punishment was the rose garden. The rose garden was a small area enclosed by barbed wire where so condemned prisoners had to stand absolutely motionless till the evening bell, which rang at none o' clock, relieved them. When, from lack of strength and sheer exhaustion someone fell down, he was kicked till he stood again, or his body had to be removed on a wheelbarrow.

After evening parade, which could take hours, the prisoners went into the barracks where they received "tea" and a piece of bread. Exhaustion brought sleep quickly. In my dreams I would compose exquisite menus of all kinds of delicacies, and I would consume gigantic mountainous servings of food.

14

This parade, however was not a normal routine parade. There was no "Nieder" and "Auf," but there was interminable counting. Time and again the prisoners in the front and at the side of the blocks had to call their numbers. After the numbers had been shouted, the S.S, would huddle and come out to start counting anew. It went on for hours, and it became clear that the count did not tally which could only mean that someone had escaped.

I had often thought about escape. With my bunkmate I had spoken about it in hushed tones. We would wait for a dark night, break one of the small windows, crawl toward the barbed wire parameter of the camp, dig a tunnel underneath the fence and vanish into the woods.

Those plan were as much fantasy as the gourmet meals I cooked at night. The windows were barred, the barracks were patrolled, and on the guard towers soldiers turned floodlights on the barbed wire around the camp. Especially during the first month of imprisonment I kept devising ever more intricate schemes of escape. I did it with the stubbornness and persistence of a pauper dreaming about unexpected windfalls of riches.

After a few months the dreams of escape ceased, dissipated in the harsh reality of my imprisonment. Silenced into nothingness like a broadcast slowly disappears from your car radio when you travel beyond the station's reach. Food, rather than escape became my obsession. My dream dinners took on gargantuan proportions in reversed ratio to my increasing hunger.

The mixture of humiliation and hunger was as poisonous as any deadly venom. It caused paralysis of the will, and it attacked somewhere in one's being the determination to survive. The first symptom was a sort of gradual withdrawal. The mind or spirit, or whatever is the core of a human being withdrew from the body. It watched the suffering as an uninvolved spectator. It looked at all the misery from a safe distance. It constructed an impenetrable fortress into which the prisoner withdrew.

The onset of these symptoms was clearly visible. Eyes staring as if they were focussed on some far away incomprehensible happening. A shuffling gait, and sometimes a vague smile on the lips.

These people would withdraw from conversations, and whatever fellowship was possible. When beaten, they would hardly react, and when cursed they would pay no attention.

It was the beginning of death. The person attending his own wake. Usually such sufferers lasted no longer than a few days. They had chosen to die, because anything worth living for had vanished from their consciousness.

I knew myself to be capable of entering that last stage of life. Often I resisted the lure of the peace of death by devising ever more glorious dinners. Fiercely I resisted within myself the temptation to let go of life.

The floodlights at the guard towers had been turned on and they cast mysterious shadows in the empty rose garden. Again we were commanded to count, and again the S.S. reported to the Sturmtrupfuhrer at the front. And time and again the count did not tally. We had stood on the parade ground for almost two hours. It was unseasonably cold, and I began to shiver.

Something was being discussed among the S.S. at the front. Finally one of the soldiers separated himself from the group and made his way to the gate. He disappeared from our sight. After half an hour he came back, accompanied, as we could see, by the camp commandant. That was bad news. We all knew the cruelty of that man.

As he approached the prisoners the command rang out; "Mutzen ab." Prisoners could not be in the presence of that exalted officer of the German Reich with heads covered. About eight hundred caps were lifted from eight hundred bald heads and pressed at the right side against the seam of the pants. Just then the moon appeared for perhaps no more than a minute

That minute was a crucial period in my life. Those sixty seconds, if that is how long it lasted, was filled literally with timeless eternity. It was the moment when the scale on which my being had so delicately been balanced between life and death, dropped decisively down on the side of life. Somewhere from depths I could not, and still cannot fathom, the knowledge that I was going to live surfaced into *my consciousness with absolute certainty. It was as if in the twinkling of an eye, in the millionth part of a micro second I became invincible. Immortal!*

What happened was that in that moment the light of the moon had broken through the clouds and bounced off eight hundred bald heads. That sight surprised me. It was a spooky sight. Surrealism in plain reality. Moonlight radiating from eight hundred bald heads. A sea of bald heads like little bulbs on a huge Christmas tree. Light from eight hundred glaringly bald skulls.

All of a sudden I realized that I was smiling. It was an almost forgotten bodily function like that of a stroke victim who regains the use of a limb. I smiled! Not only did I smile, I had trouble not bursting into laud laughter. The sight of those eight hundred bald heads reflecting the light of the moon was so utterly ridiculous.

In the total and absolute absurdity of that moment I regained the connection with life. I was born again in a smile. Life took hold of me anew, and its grip was firmer than ever before. It held me like a lover holds the beloved, never to let go.

We stood there until close to noon. Patrols of S.S. soldiers inspected the barracks. Other detachments left to search the surrounding woods. It was by now beyond any shadow of a doubt that at least one prisoner had escaped. He must have made it for an earlier attempt had resulted in a similar parade with one difference: the escapee was brought back and beaten to death in front of the assembled camp population.

People began to faint in the blocks of prisoners. As their number increased we were dismissed and sent back to the barracks. On the way back I supported someone who was stumbling. He looked as if he was about to die. I put him on my bunk, and went to get some water for him. When I came back he was gone. I had forgotten to look at his number. I don't know whether he survived. I did because I found life in a smile.

Exodus 15 : 22-16 : 10

How good is life in Elim! Twelve springs of water no less. The whole oasis is filled with the goodness of God. There is sufficient water for men and beast, and not a discouraging word is heard.

Here men sing their silent doxologies and women smile at the sight of children playing in the sand. The old rest their weary limbs, and everybody soaks in the peace and rest of life in Elim. The place stirs deeply buried memories of stories about paradise. God is in heaven and all is well. It is that kind of place and that kind of time.

At night the soothing sound of pipe and timbrel mix with the rustling of the wind through the palm trees. Delight is visible on the faces of the people, and when the fires burn at night the parents tell their children of God's deeds.

"I am the Lord your healer," God had said when they came to Elim. God heals the wounds of his people in Elim. Stiff from traveling, sore from past injuries, and scarred by terrifying fears, their journey has now brought them to Elim. "I am the Lord your healer," then they came to Elim where there were twelve springs of water and—count them well—seventy palm trees.

So God leads his people from the terror of being caught between the sea and the Egyptians, with death staring them in the face, and he brings them into the peace and rest of Elim. This is for God's people time to gather strength. Time to restore the soul. The words of Psalm 23 come to mind: "He leads me beside quiet waters." In the shadow of the seventy palm trees life is good.

Every one who experiences such rest and tranquility at whatever place or whatever time would like to perpetuate those periods. On the Mount of Tranfiguration in the blessed presence of Jesus. Moses and Elijah; Peter said it: "Lord it is well that we are here, if you wish I will make three tents, one for you, and one for Moses and one for Elijah."

How much would we all like to stay in Elim! Placid in the coolness of the shadow. Life sweet and undisturbed. Fountains of water to quench our thirst. And above the fountains brilliant stars that make the darkness seem light. We all know those times and those places, and we have prayed: "Lord let me stay here. Lord let me build my house in Elim." No pain, no sorrow, no worry, only goodness and mercy.

Deep within us stirs the longing for paradise lost. Somewhere in our being we can still touch the memory of Eden's peace. Elim is as close as we can get. Elim is where we sing our doxologies for God's grace and goodness. It is as close as we can get to paradise. It is the oasis of God's healing. Alas we know also that Elim is at the edge of the wilderness. The Lord who is our healer, and who guides us to Elim, is also the God who told his people to depart from Elim and set foot again in the desert.

He did it to his only begotten Son, Jesus the Christ. Jesus was led by the Spirit into the wilderness to be tempted by the devil. The wilderness is the place of our temptation. No sooner has the shape of Elim's palm trees vanished behind the horizon or hunger and thirst make their re-appearance. Led into the wilderness, God's people seem to lose their trust and their hope in God. Their faith vanishes at the first sign of trouble like mist in the morning sun.

Hear them protesting and complaining: "Would that we had died by the hand of the Lord in the land of Egypt, when we sat around pots of meat and ate all the food we wanted, but you have brought us out into the wilderness to starve this entire assembly to death."

Like the sight of Elim's palm trees disappeared from the view of the people, so they abandoned their trust in God.It evaporated in the trouble and pain of the desert.

The doxologies are forgotten and cussing and swearing took their place. When the blessing of Elim became no more than a memory, the weariness of wilderness-living brought on rebellion and complaint.

Most of us are at one time or another led into the wilderness of temptation. It happens. Coming from Elim one might unexpectedly and suddenly wind up in the wilderness. We call it suffering. The Bible calls it temptation. Now in the wilderness can you hang on to your faith? Can you continue to confess God the healer who will restore your soul for his name's sake? In the wilderness can you keep on hoping in God?

We read in the previous chapter how Paul and Silas were thrown in that dungeon. They were beaten with rods, inflicted with many blows, their feet shackled. Yet we read in Acts 16 verse 25: "About midnight Paul and Silas were praying and singing hymns to God…"

The Israelites sang their own peculiar hymns in the wilderness. God how can you do this to us? God you don't look after us anymore. You have forsaken us. God don't you care for your people?

See how temptation confronts us in the wilderness of our lives. Whether it is between Elim and Sinai, or in the cancer ward of the hospital, in the parched dryness of arid land, or in the wilderness of a disintegrating marriage, or in the pain and sorrow of broken ideals and shattered dreams; there will be the temptation of giving up hope. I faced that temptation in a German concentration camp.

In the wilderness you meet people clubbed down by the harshness of life, robbed of happiness, and beaten down by the cruel events of their existence. Yes it is suffering, but it is also temptation. Can you hold on to God? Can you hope in the Lord to renew your strength? Can you believe in God's goodness even in the wilderness? Can you remember Elim and make the words of psalm 42 your own: I shall yet praise him?

Our question in the wilderness is—why. Why does this happen to me? Why must I go through this? The Bible poses a different question and creates a different suspense: Can he, can she keep the faith?

Strung up as it were between the ambiguities of our existence, living in that mixture of goodness and evil, knowing God's goodness and grace, yet experiencing the agony of the wilderness can you persist in faith?

Let us focus on verse ten of Exodus sixteen: "While Aaron was speaking for the whole Israelite community, they looked toward the desert, and there was the glory of the Lord appearing in the cloud."

All too often we believe that God is only in Elim. The God of prosperity and health and riches and success. But see! Discover! Look! There in the wilderness appeared the glory of God. He is present in the wilderness of life. How could we ever think that he would fail us. Listen to his promise to the Israelites: at twilight you will eat meat, and in the morning you will be filled with bread."

When I lay my own life beside this text I must confess that it was in the wilderness of my life, in a sea of suffering that I saw the glory of God's presence and I experienced it more vividly, more real than in most Elim periods.

Many a Christian will testify that when he or she was taken from the rest and peace of Elim, and led into the wilderness, they gathered strength because of a heightened sense of God's presence. Many will even go further and confess that it was good for them that God brought them from Elim into the wilderness for it was there that they experienced his presence and his strength as never before.

In the Book of Ecclesiastes, in chapter seven verse two, the preacher says: "It is better to go to a house of mourning than to go to a house of feasting." He too must have experienced God's presence in bad times. More even than in times of feasting. That ancient preacher expresses what becomes clear in this Exodus Bible passage: God can be missed in Elim, but you will find him in the wilderness.

Please note this and let it be anchored in your memory that not in Elim, but in the wilderness the glory of God became visible to the people. I am sure that the apostle James knew of God's glory in the wilderness, for this he wrote: "Consider it pure joy, my brothers, whenever you face trials of many kinds."(James 1:2)

At first glance statements like that do not seem to make sense. It escapes comprehension. Joy and in suffering and trials, it sounds insane. But if you have been there, like Paul and Silas, like concentration camp survivors, like the people of Israel, and you have been blessed with the vision, the experience of the glory of God's glorious presence then it makes sense. Then it dawns on you that there truly is a peace which surpasses understanding. Peace even in the wilderness.

Yes the Exodus passage refers to a definite experience and vision of that glory of God: the cloud. It is not in that way that God makes his presence known to us. "In the past God spoke to our forefathers through the prophets at many times and in various ways, but in these last days he has spoken to us by his Son." (Hebrews 1:1) That Son himself was led into the wilderness to be tempted. It is his promise which comes alive especially in the wilderness: "And surely I am with you always, to the very end of the age."

Carry the words of this Bible passage in your heart: "I am the Lord your healer." He will be with you in Elim and in the wilderness and guide us all to where the wilderness will be forever gone in the new Jerusalem, which is irrigated by the river of the water of life.

CHAPTER THREE
LET THE CHILDREN COME

I sit down on the bench in the back of the pulpit. Silence is not obtained easily in a full church. Someone clears his throat. There is the sound of shuffling feet, and rasping coughs echo through the sanctuary. After a few moments I become aware of absence of sounds. Soon silence fills the space. I turn my thoughts loose. Years float by like wind-driven clouds over a hilltop. Images come in focus in rapid succession, only to be replaced by other shapes and forms. At times something lingers....

The hour is early, very early. Darkness has given up its grip on the coming day, but it still hides the horizon from my view.

Snow covers the ground. Trees stand leafless, bending in the wind. It is bitterly cold.

A sound reaches my ear. It is the sound of thousands of feet marching over the hard frozen ground. The sound, as yet separated from sight of the approaching people, creates a ghostly impression. It mixes with the whistling of the wind into a scary noise.

In the distance I begin to see a long snake-like form. It is a column of prisoners. As they approach I see their blue-striped uniforms. Their breath makes little clouds in the cold air. Armed guards surround them. When they come closer I see faces in the front row, and with amazement I see that there are children in that first row. Their eyes are hollow, and the cheekbones jut sharply in their faces. Their heads are bald and uncovered, their hands bare.

One of the little one stumbles and falls. People in the following row falter in their walk, and I see some hands reaching out trying to lift the little one. The air explodes with rough-sounding German curses. Guards jump into the column beating and kicking the prisoners. A momentary flailing of riflebutts, and the steady pace of walking resumes. There is an empty spot in the first row. I watch the whole column pass by. It seems an interminable flow of marchers. Finally the last row passes by, and there remains in the middle of the road the stretched-out body of a child. The snow around the body is red. No one looks backward. It is as if someone had dropped something of no value like an empty book of matches that presently will be swept up by street cleaners.

I feel a dull pain of hopeless sorrow, a sadness beyond tears, and the companionship of death.

LUKE 18:15-17

Luke tells us that people brought their children to Jesus in spite of the disciples' rebuke. Jesus gladly acceded to the request of prayers and blessing for the little children. The happening is described with slightly different nuances In Matthew, Mark and Luke. It receives a lot of emphasis in the Bible.

In the passage the anti-child attitude of the disciples is rebuked by the Lord, in whom the pro-child grace of God is visible and children are held up as an example to us all. Anti-child, pro-child and children as an example. Three observations from the text.

Let us see the scene as the Bible passage describes it. Jesus and the disciples travel toward Jerusalem. On their way they pass through the countryside. They meet different groups of people. Ten lepers are healed during this journey. Jesus teaches lessons about the coming of the kingdom. He tells a parable about prayer. A wonderful story about a persistent widow and a non-caring judge.

Then there is the parable about the Pharisee and the tax collector. That parable has that unexpected ending with the tax collector going home justified and the law abiding Pharisee staying—so to say—in the cold of his own confidence.

From looking at the context, here as well as in the other gospels,

I think, although I am not altogether sure about that, that Jesus and the disciples have arrived in Jerusalem, and that they are in or close to the temple court.

Then babies are brought to Jesus. There is a popular song which says that women did that. The writers of that song probably imagined that if babies were brought to Jesus, it must have been the mothers who did that. In none of the there gospels, however is it said that the babies were brought by their mothers. They might have been brought by their grandfathers, or who knows by whom.

These were very small children. Children who could not yet walk. Babies who still nursed. People brought these babies to Jesus with the request that he would touch them and pray for them.

The people in this passage are not received kindly by the disciples who turn on them with rebuke. Faultfinding. Disapproval. Sharp criticism. Get out of here! And we really don't know what the reason is for this rejection. Everybody speculates why the disciples do that, and many come up with different reasons. None of the gospels tell us why it happened. But we clearly see here something that is not limited to the time and the world of the disciples. There is in many countries an anti-child attitude that has accompanied humankind in history and has become quite pronounced in our time.

There is an almost world-wide anti-child societal climate. The increase in abortions could be one of the symptoms of such an attitude. Hundred and thousands of children in this world and in this time suffer from hunger and malnutrition. In Palestine children who ought to be busy learning the tables of multiplication are recruited to wage war. Drug addicted women give birth to babies who are junkies as soon as they leave the womb. Cigarette companies profit from the addiction of children. The rate of teenagers committing suicide, especially among aboriginal people, is climbing at an alarming rate. The governments of some countries export children at a large scale, and we are only beginning to see the tip of the iceberg called child abuse.

The disciples weren't the first ones to show this anti-child inclination, and they certainly haven't been the last. Look now at

Jesus, who in his humanity mysteriously is the second person of the Trinity. He truly reveals the Father to us. He saw what the disciples did, and he heard what they said. He was—so says the Gospel of Mark—indignant. Angry. Angrily upset. Sorely displeased. Jesus became very upset with what the disciples did.

Let the little children come to me. Jesus' invitation goes much further than the babies who were being turned away by the disciples. God loves children. There is a very moving story in the Old Testament. It is an Abraham and Sarai story. Both of them got tired of waiting for the fulfilment of God's promise to them. Sarai would become pregnant, God had said. But for Abraham and Sarai it took too long. So—you might remember—Abraham impregnated Hagar and Ishmael was born.

Of course the Lord did not go back on his promise. He never does, and in God's own time Abraham and Sarai received their son Isaac. It was then that the trouble in that household started. Sarai demanded that Abraham send Hagar and her son away. Get rid of them. And so, Abraham did a very cruel thing. He chased both Hagar and Ishmael into the desert, where death by dehydration almost certainly awaited them.

After some days Hagar was exhausted and near to death. She laid Ishmael in the shade of some shrubbery. She went a little further because she did not want to see her son die. And then it says in Genesis 21:17 "God heard the boy crying." It is one of those little phrases, just a few words, that say so much about God our Father. Think about it: "God heard the boy crying." And God provided water both for Hagar and Ishmael. Those five words—God heard the boy crying—reveal so much about God. As a matter of fact those five words tell us as much, if not more about God, than any five books of systematic theology. God heard the boy crying. God hears the cry of children.

There is another part of the Bible that speaks of God's care for children. It is in the Book of Jonah, the last chapter. Nineveh has repented and turned to God. And then it says: God had compassion, and did not bring upon them the destruction he had threatened.

Jonah, as you remember, was not very pleased with that turn of events. He had looked forward to the ruin of the city. He was mightily displeased that the show was cancelled.

And then God teaches Jonah and us all a great lesson about his compassion. The Lord said: "Nineveh has more than a hundred and twenty thousand people who cannot tell their right hand from their left, should I not be concerned about that great city?"

One hundred and twenty thousand who could not tell their right hand from their left. Those are children aren't they? Of course they are. God's compassion and care and concern had to do with that vast amount of children in the city.

And the Bible is emphatic also about God's special care for orphans. The fatherless, the Old Testament calls them. The little people who had no provider anymore. God made the whole nation responsible for the welfare of the widows and the fatherless. God was greatly concerned about them. As a matter of fact, James the brother of Jesus writes in his epistle: "Religion that God accepts as pure and faultless is this—to look after orphans and widows in their distress."

And in our passage from the Gospel of Luke is the incarnated word of God. God himself in Jesus Christ. We hear it clearly from his mouth: "Let the children come to me and do not hinder them". And Matthew records a warning that Jesus added: "See that you do not look down on one of these little ones for I tell you that their angels in heaven always see the face of my Father in heaven." Again there we see that special care of God for children. Those who minister to children are very clearly doing a kind of work that is very dear and precious in God's eyes.

The passage also shows that Jesus holds up children as an example to us. "I tell you the truth, anyone who will not receive the kingdom of God like a little child will never enter it."

Jesus says that with respect to our relationship with God, children are exemplary. Children are our examples. Nobody knows what Jesus exactly meant with those words. What exactly in children— Jesus uses there the word that indicates more than just babies—what in those children is exemplary for our relationship with God. Children, and no parent would ever want to deny that, can be very cruel, self-centred and sometimes they drive their parents up the wall. Yes, as somebody said: sometimes they are what you call a great monumental pain in the neck.

What then does Jesus refer to in children when he holds them up to s as examples? No one can be absolutely sure what particular characteristic of children Jesus refers to, but with the help of the context we can make a fairly good guess.

Just before this happening Luke records the parable of the Pharisee and the tax collector who both were praying. The Pharisee presented his most excellent religious resume: tithing, fasting, all kinds of good stuff. God here I am, your most worthy servant whom you must really be pleased to count among your people, and for whom certainly the red carpet must be rolled out. And there is also the tax collector: no merit points, no golden stars behind his name. A despicable sort of fellow. Everybody despised his kind. And somehow the man knew as he faced God in his prayer that there wasn't much else he could do than plead for mercy. Beg. And Jesus said: "I tell you that this man rather than the other went home justified before God."

And then precisely in that context Luke remembers this episode about the children being held up as an example by the Lord. There is a strong pointer then to the fact that Jesus probably had reference to the children's ability to ask. Any parent or grandparent can tell that one of the great talents of children—a talent that they use freely and frequently—is their ability to ask and keep asking. Can I have this? Can I do that? Who knows how many times day.

See there is our example: we have to learn to live by grace. Leave our religious brownie points in our pocket. Don't send in a resume filled with good deeds. Don't expect a star behind your name in the book of life. We must know again that all we can do is what the tax collector of Jesus' parable did: "God have mercy on me a sinner."

It was Martin Luther's last lesson which he taught with his last breath: "Wir sint Bittler." We are all beggars.

CHAPTER FOUR
DEAD MAN COUNTED

He was a gentleman of distinction. He dressed like all of us in the dirty camp-uniform, yet something in his person, the way he spoke and looked and behaved made him stand out. An aura of importance clung to him, yet his manner of spirit did not convey arrogance, rather kindness and compassion.

He spoke with the intonation and cadence that betrayed erudition, yet his words never expressed the hauteur that people who speak that way sometimes convey. He wore the yellow star of David, which all Jews were required to wear, as a badge of dishonour. He had a long beard since Jews were not allowed to shave. I don't remember his number, and I never knew his name, yet his face appears from time to time in my memory.

Even the S.S. soldiers noticed that he was no ordinary prisoner. They ridiculed him and beat him more frequently than they did others. One of the blond brutes once lifted him by his beard which must have caused the man excruciating pain.

As often happened to Jewish prisoners, this one day two S.S. men marked him for death. Already early in the morning they began to follow him and beat him mercilessly. When he fell down they kicked him up again. One of the savages lit a match and burnt the man's beard. Blood streamed from his face where the skin had been burned off.

We of the Jewish kommando, as our block of prisoners was called, carried bricks on large wooden trays from one end of the camp to the other end. Poles stuck out on each end of the trays so that two men could carry them. When all the bricks had been carried to one end of the camp we would have to start the whole process in reverse. All the time the S.S. men would yell that the trays were not loaded full enough or that we did not walk fast enough.

Everyone knew that this was the last day for our fellow prisoner. A deadly silence settled among the men of the kommando. Only the curses of the S.S. soldiers rang out in the air. It was as if we ourselves felt the pain of the kicks and beatings. There was the heavy anticipation of a common grief to be borne. It must have been around eleven o'clock in the morning when he stumbled again, and no amount of kicking by the guards got him up. He had fallen for the last time. They let him lie on the sand. That's where he died shortly before the noon hour for his body was brought in on a wheelbarrow for the count.

Dead, but still included in the count. Dead or alive, all present and accounted for! So are God's people in His count. Job knew it.

Job 19 : 25

I have seen Job, and I have heard him. I saw him in that infamous striped pyjama uniform of concentration camp inmates. I heard him moan when he was close to death a long time ago in a concentration camp. I am sure that he mixed his moaning with prayer for I hear him speak words. I did not understand what he was praying, but he must have committed his soul unto God, for he, and we all, knew that he was going to die.

I was only a young man when I met Job, not very much occupied with philosophical or theological questions, rather totally absorbed in trying to stay alive, yet I do remember asking myself how all that fitted into the faintly remembered catechism lessons of God is good.

That question has stayed with me. I keep looking for an answer like someone who lost the last piece of his jigsaw puzzle. There is that hole in the picture that you cannot fill. Job's friends of course thought that they had found the missing piece. They had completed the puzzle of Job's suffering. Their picture was complete with all the pieces nicely fitting together. Job you might as well accept it: God is zapping you with his anger. God is unfurling his wrath. There is some skeleton in your closet that you haven't told us, but God knows where it is, and you are now being punished.

Easy as pie, no theological treatise necessary, no need for apologetics, it is simply this: God is taking revenge. What is happening here is that God is pouncing on a big sinner with big punishment. With friends like that why would Job need enemies. There are always friends who have these easy explanations of suffering. There are always people who come running along with a bunch of Bible texts. There are always people who know exactly what God is doing and therefore have all the answers. I have seen and heard them especially in the reception rooms of funeral parlours where they held forth with what they thought was comfort and consolation.

Job and all his fellow sufferers are really not consoled by these efforts. Look at Job's friends, like early Freudian psychoanalysts they pry into his life, digging like prospectors for some sin that would explain it all.

By the way, between brackets here and as an aside, what really surprised many people and even made people angry is that when God came to live on this earth he did not zap sinners, but in utter amazement the Gospels say, he visited with them, he ate with them, attended their parties and forgave their sins.

Returning to Job we read that he does not accept the easy explanations of his friends. It is not I who have wronged God, but God has wronged me. That does not make it any easier as a matter of fact that is the deepest pain of Job's suffering. God what do you have against me. Why is all this happening to me.

Look at me, feel my pain. I heard In Job's lament already the distant cry of one who asked the same question: My God, my God why have you forsaken me.

Reading and reading again, it seemed to me that all of Job's material losses were not the deepest suffering. It is almost as if the Bible says that is not the worst. In a sort of off-handed way at the end of the story it is mentioned that Job became rich again, that his business grew beyond that what he had before all this happened to him. Seven sons and three daughters.

Awful though his losses were, inexpressibly painful and agonizing, I hear the deepest torment of his distress in the fact that the cry—why have you forsaken me—does not get an answer. There it is that the book of Job touches our life.

We don't get answers when a young child dies from leukemia, or when the smoke curled up through the chimneys of the death camps. We don't get an answer when…. and you may fill in the details of the suffering, the sorrow and the disillusions you have seen and witnessed.

Job's wife could not live with that vacuum of unanswered questions. She gave up on God. Ditch it all—this God business, I have had it. Her complaint is really bottled up honesty. I have had it with you God. I once sat in an airplane next to a Jewish gentleman. He asked me what I did for a living, and I told him that I was a minister. That immediately brought up the "Why," and the man told me with disappointment almost audible in his voice that he could not believe in God anymore. He is not alone of course. Especially in Europe the church is decimated of membership almost beyond recognition. Big cathedral-like buildings with on Sunday a few pews filled with ever older people. I wonder whether it has to do with the fact that no answer could ever explain the ravages and the suffering of World War II.

Our text for this morning shows a different reaction: "I know that my redeemer lives." Handel incorporated it in his Messiah with that hauntingly beautiful aria "I know that my redeemer liveth." Catch that word redeemer. It implies that something has to be corrected or restored. Redeemers in Israel were often close kinfolk who would help you in very bitter circumstances. Redeemers were people who would bail you out when you had hit rock bottom.

And listen again to Job: "I know that my redeemer lives." Listen sharply. Like the sound of some distant music, audible only vaguely, yet clearly discernable is the tone of hope: "I know that my redeemer lives." There is yet a way out. There is still an open door. There is still hope. I am not totally collapsing. I can still look ahead and see more than the darkness in which I am wrapped up now. I know that my redeemer lives, the door to the future is still ajar.

The opposite of the reaction of Job' wife. Faith born in and out of suffering. Growth in sorrow. Sometimes I believe that without pain the growth of faith is stunted. It is often in pain that by grace we grow spiritually. I once read how the hymn "Peace like a River" came about. This man Stafford saw his wife and I believe three daughters off on their journey to England. He would follow them later. The ship on which his wife and daughters sailed met with disaster, it sank and Stafford's daughters drowned. His wife was rescued and she cabled him from England. He set sail immediately to join her, and when his ship sailed in the vicinity where his daughters had lost their lives, he went downstairs into his cabin and wrote the hymn called: "Peace like a River."

"When sorrow like sea billows roll, whatever my lot, thou hast taught me to say: it is well with my soul." It is almost like Job's stubborn clinging to faith: "I know that my redeemer lives."

During the seventies I visited in St. Margaret's Hospital in Toronto. Cancer patients were cared for in that hospital. I met pain, suffering and agony, but also spiritual riches, and trust, and often Job's expression of hope: "I know that my redeemer lives."

Job's exclamation is God's invitation to see the open door of the future in whatever circumstances of life. Is that perhaps why Paul says give thanks in all circumstances? It struck me at one time that he did not say for all circumstances, but in all circumstances. In all circumstances there is still an open door to the future: the redeemer.

Listen with me also to the personal pronoun. I know that my redeemer lives. Hear the closeness. My redeemer. This is no long distance relationship. Not just any redeemer, no theoretical philosophical redeemer. This is my redeemer.

For years, no for centuries, the church has been enriched by the words of the apostolic creed. I believe in God the father. The father! There are not that many atheists, I think. Most people believe in something out there or up there. A God as a distant star, a God at arms length. God out there. But God himself does not want to be at a distance. One of the most moving parts in the Bible is in Hosea 11 where God pleads to be Israel's personal God. "I taught you to walk," he says, "I took you in my arms, I led them with cords of kindness and love. I am your redeemer."

Look again at our text, listen to Job again The chips for this Job were down further than we can imagine. Everything is gone. Family, business, friends, health all is gone. Philosophy is not much help to him. This is no time for parlour psychology. He reaches out to the only thing, no not thing, the only person that is left and he wrings from his tortured soul the last but bottom line confession: "I know that my redeemer lives."

Once more hear that word redeemer. You know what it signifies. Someone, a close relative who will bail you out when you are down. I think that Job here stares death in the face. In verse twenty three he wishes that he could leave the world a testament of his innocence written in stone. "Engraved on a rock forever," he says. I am a goner he must have thought, and his personal faith reaches beyond death a redeemer who will in the end declare Job to be innocent.

We know him, Job's redeemer. His life's journey too was a way of suffering, he was despised and rejected. Yet the Bible calls us also to look beyond his suffering to the great deed of salvation and grace the resurrection. His lament: "Why have you forsaken me?" found its answer on that third day.

In Jesus' resurrection Job's hope of a coming redeemer is realized. There is one who rose above all suffering and agony and in whose triumph Job will share. In Jesus Christ God tell us Job was right: his redeemer lives. Don't leave it there.

Your redeemer too lives.

Job's suffering has accompanied the history of people. The sound of that Hebrew prayer intoned by a dying man was an echo of past suffering. It was the voice of the man's terrible agony, and at the same time a prophecy of the future pain and misery of mankind.

Once in a while I can still hear it. Time flies, but memory stands still. A warm summer day. The sand hot and bright yellow under my feet and him lying there. Dying like an animal on the ground. Raw, loud guttoral shouts of the guards, and then rising from the misery that indescribable moaning sound of a prayer.

I don't know what he prayed—God will know that—he was one of his people. But the sound of that prayer offered and spoken de profundis goes on through the world and through our history. Job lives on. You meet him in hospitals, in Lourdes in France where he had gone to seek healing and had not found it, in war-stricken cities where houses lie in ruins, in any family where word is received word that a son had been killed in battle, where he mourns disappeared children and in cemeteries where he came to lay flowers on the grave of his wife.

And for him, he whose God is the personal God of salvation there is in all of that the accompanying promise of God: know that your redeemer lives.

CHAPTER FIVE
THE WAIL THAT ECHOES

Memory is a selective sadist. Cruelly it robs a person of riches that one would like to treasure, yet like a miser holding on to his money, it also forces one to preserve lots of very disagreeable ugliness. It deposited a sound in my head that I cannot get rid of. The picture that goes with it is faded, but it still has enough shape to add to the recurrent disquieting echo in my mind.

I don't know what time of the year it is, except that it is not winter. There is no snow on the ground. I stand under trees which already or yet bear leaves. Not far away from me, no more than a hundred or so yards, a truck is being loaded with people. They must be newly arrived prisoners for they do not wear the blue striped camp uniform.

As they climb into the truck every one of them is being kicked in by one of the guards that stand around. The guards take turns kicking. The prisoners sit on the two sides of the truck and lots of them on the floor in the middle. When it seems that there is no more room the guards kick a few more men into the truck. They land on top of the ones already there.

One guard lifts the back gate into place and signals to the driver. Just as the truck is about to start a muffled sound rises out of its bed. It surprises me for it is a song, sung by a chorus of a truckload of men. I do not recognise the language, but it must be Hebrew. These are Jews, and I know where Jewish prisoners are going.

There is no joy in the song. It has a sort of repetitive cadence to it. A low-toned lament in rhythm. It carries a multitude of suffering, as if the pains of generations have been distilled in this one melody of affliction. Encapsulated in the chorus is the agony of ages. Centuries of pain have settled in a three-ton truck.

As the truck drives beyond my sight around a bend in the road, I keep hearing the sound. Even now, years later when the truck has long gone and disintegrated, and its load of people have entered eternity, that ballad of torment clings to my soul.

It pops up at unexpected moments like hail in summertime. It comes and goes with irregular intervals, but it is never totally out of earshot. The truck keeps turning a bend in the road and the singing continues. Sometimes I can hear its faint hum in a far away crevice of my mind, but it can also come in on high volume.

Wherever or whenever it appears in my hearing it always comes wrapped in profound sadness. Grief cleaves to it inseparably. I hear it is as if it harmonizes with the Golgotha cry: "My God why have you forsaken me." There is an anguish to it that is unspeakable. Woe beyond words. Perhaps a descent into hell. I want to lose it, but memory won't let me.

Genesis 35: 16-20
Jeremiah 31: 15-17
Matthew 2: 16-18

Her short life, she died giving birth, was not filled with a lot of delight. Her days were spent in storm and strife. Rachel was her name and her father sold her to her cousin for seven years of labour. With her wedding to him she became a member of a very dysfunctional family. Cousin Jacob had another wife beside her and he also sired children with two additional women. To add to her misery Rachel remained childless while Leah, the other wife, gave birth to sons like clockwork hoping that her fertility would gain her the love of Jacob. First there was Reuben, then Simeon, and then Levi and Judah.

While all that was happening Rachel's pain and misery is described in three words: "Rachel was barren." And sibling rivalry does not even begin to describe Rachel's adversary relationship with her sister. Her father Laban apparently passed on some very disagreeable genes to his daughters. They were cunning and often sneaky women ready to pull a fast one if that would suit their purposes. And Jacob himself wasn't above some crafty shenanigans either. What a family!

But Rachel was really hurting. Infertility was a shame. A curse looked upon as a punishment from God. At one time Rachel was so desperate and almost suicidal about it that she said to Jacob: "Give me children or I die." There wasn't much happiness in Rachel's life. A nomadic existence, having to compete with her rival sister who gave her husband sons and feeling ashamed of her infertility. Not the stuff for a sugar sweet romance novel. On the contrary a life filled with tragedy.

What a joy it must have been when finally she too bore a son: Joseph. God has taken away my disgrace she said and she called her son Joseph. Once more she became pregnant and she bore another son but she died in childbirth not before with her last breath she named the baby Benoni. Son of sorrows.

The name of that little boy summed up Rachel's life. Sorrow, pain and misery. Jacob though would not let his son go through his days with a constant reminder of his mother's tragic life. He renamed Benoni and called him Benjamin, son of the south. The south stood for all that was good and pleasant. The son of sorrow became the son of the south, son of pleasure and goodness. I don't know why Jacob renamed that child. Maybe his trust in the future did it, maybe his faith in God the provider, I don't really know.

But now hear what I hear: Rachel's lament. My life sorrow. My child my son, son of my sorrow. Benoni is a scream of pain and disillusion, a wail that travels through the Bible.

For come with me who knows how many years later. The time of Jeremiah whose life was no picnic either. A poet by nature, God called him to be a prophet. The time is about 580 before Christ. History is repeating itself. She, who so passionately longed for children, has in a sense become childless again. Her children, the people of Israel are in exile. And listen: this is what Jeremiah heard the Lord say: "A voice is heard in Ramah mourning and great weeping Rachel weeping for her children and refusing to be comforted."

Still today there is in Ramah a tomb honored by Christians, Jews and Muslims as Rachel's burying place. It is only probable that this tomb monument marks the right spot of Rachel's grave. But in this part of our Jeremiah passage it does say her wail is heard in Ramah. Why Ramah?

Ramah was a transit camp from which the people were driven to Babylon. Thousands men and women and children, not knowing what the future would hold. Anxious, worried, driven from home, and now captives of the enemy—the Babylonians. A scene reminiscent of W.W. II camps in Europe from where Jewish people were sent to Auschwitz and other hellish places. I have seen and lived in those portals of hell.

There are no words to describe the misery and the pain of those places. There is no better way to touch the terrible torture of the people in Jeremiah's time than to listen with the ears of your heart and soul and hear the lament of Rachel—this time in plural. Sons of my sorrow.

Whoever listens that way could indeed hear Rachel's wail again in and around Hitler's murder camps. Not only there. Rachel's wail has accompanied all the history of God's people. And when I say God's people I include all of God's people. All those who are God's children. Listen even now with the ear that can stab through the layer of ages and hear again Rachel's wail. It did not only echo along the path of Israel's history, but it sounded over all the battlefields of the world from Thermopelea to the World Trade Center. Her children were no more.

And yet there is another cry. Above Rachel's wail Jeremiah heard again the voice of the Lord saying "Restrain your voice from weeping, and your eyes from tears. They will return from the land of the enemy so there is hope for the future."

Can you hear that voice too? You-we-living in the shadow of Cain with the terror of the concentration camps settled still raw in our memory like an ulcer on the flesh. The miserable memory of that horror-like bitter wormwood in our mouth. Can we hear what Jeremiah heard? When Rachel's cry echoes amid the skyscrapers of New York City or in the refugee camps in Pakistan can you hear the other voice? "There is hope for the future."

We often are deaf to that other voice that accompanies Rachel's wail. Her lament is expressive of so much blood-curling evil that the other voice is often drowned out. Yet Jeremiah heard it, the children of Israel were invited to hear it, and we are invited to hear it: there is hope for the future.

Come with me to yet again another time. The time of Herod the King. The name Herod has some connotation of heroism but we know that this particular Herod—there were more than one in Israel's history—was no hero. When he heard rumours of a potential competitor to the throne being born he sent out the death squad. In order to be sure that no threat would come from Bethlehem he sent his murdering soldiers to that little town with the order to kill all the boys up to two years old.

And Matthew when he told the story to his Jewish compatriots heard Rachel's wail again. The echo of that terrible pain-filled cry that first sounded in Jacob's tent Benoni. Children of my sorrows, was heard again in Ramah and then sounded in Bethlehem. Benoni. Son of my pain, my children of sorrow.

But as I said that scream of sorrow did not only sound over the misery of Jacob's family, over the horror of Camp Ramah or in Bethlehem over the shrieks of little boys dying at the hand of Roman soldiers. Listen at Remembrance Day, listen during that minute of silence and you can hear it again; Rachel's wail. Children of my sorrow.

Listen in the silence of any moment, or in the music you happen to hear. The 1812 overture of Tzaikovsky, the ninth symphony of Beethoven, and others. There is that painting called Scream. I saw the sculpture of uplifted arms where the old city of Rotterdam was bombed into ruins, and I heard Rachel's wail. Walk the war cemeteries and read the names of young men, nineteen twenty years old. Children killed like a million leafs blown from a tree by the autumn wind, and hear again the sobbing heard in Ramah. Rachel weeping and refusing to be comforted.

Matthew heard Rachel's wail in the murder of the innocent in Bethlehem. No he did not add the other voice that Jeremiah heard. The voice that said in spite of Rachel's sorrow, there is hope for the future. Matthew did not quote the call to have hope that we read in that text of the Book of Jeremiah.

And yet that voice that Jeremiah heard is there: there is hope for the future. There is that voice. No it is not spoken. There is no oral articulation. But the voice is there: the word has become flesh. God in a tiny baby. Certainly in his body he is a son of Rachel's sorrow. A true Benoni. Isaiah already knew it: he had no beauty or majesty to attract us to him, he was despised and rejected by men, a man of sorrows and familiar with suffering.

He truly is Rachel's son Benoni. A man of sorrows. He lives in his flesh and blood Rachel's lament. Ask his mother who stood at the foot of the cross upon which he was nailed. Yet whoever watches whatever happened there in Bethlehem can also hear Joseph's reach into the future: not Benoni, son of sorrow, but Benjamin son of the south, son of goodness,

The word heard by Jeremiah "There is hope for the future" did take on human flesh in Jesus. I want us all to hear that word again, personified as it was in Jesus. There is hope for the future.

Not only did he embody that voice of God, but he affirmed it for us all: I am the first and the last, I am the living one, I was dead and behold I am alive for ever and ever, and I hold the keys of death and Hades.

And he changed the course of human history. In him God the creator started the march to the time when Rachel's wail shall be silenced for ever. He will wipe Rachel's tears from her eyes, turn her sighs into songs. When there will be no more death or mourning or crying or pain, for the old order if things will have passed away.

I hope that old Joseph in that name change from Benoni to Benjamin did a bit more than just express some optimism. Perhaps unwittingly he became a prophet by carrying within himself the ache of mankind's longing and perhaps his words reached forward to the great man of sorrows who indeed became Benjamin: son of goodness,

Optimism is hard to come by these days. So it was in the days of Jeremiah. Rachel's wail drowned out any other voice in that Camp Ramah. Yet Jeremiah heard it: "There is hope for the future." I hope you can hear it too, even over Rachel's wail.

CHAPTER SIX
THE DREAD OF DARKNESS

I don't know how it happened but my bike went off the path. I had confiscated the bike from some German who himself had probably expropriated it from a Dutch citizen By pedalling across the country, about two hundred kilometres, I hoped to reach safety before dawn. Daylight would bring the risk of being arrested again. I had biked already for a few hours when all of a sudden a cloud covered what little moonlight there had been. I lost track of the bicycle path. I fell on soft earth, but I held on to my bicycle.

It was dark. So dark that I could hardly see a hand held before my eyes. I had never experienced darkness like it. I shuffled my feet over what seemed to be grass, expecting to find the pavement again. All I felt under my feet though was grass or some other vegetation. I don't know how long I searched for hard surface so that I could jump on my bicycle again. It seemed a long time.

Fear fell upon me with a sudden rush. The dread of being captured was one part of my consternation, but being lost in utter darkness brought me close to panic. Darkness held me in its grip with a tightness that isolated me totally from my surroundings. I felt wrapped in an impenetrable veil. I continued to search with my feet since my eyes were useless. Shuffle left, shuffle right, forward and backward but I did not find solid ground.

There was something in that total darkness that terrified me. Thinking back about it I can still touch the fear that overpowered me. It took all of my willpower to remain rational and not to surrender to incoherent panic. I stopped shuffling, and started a discussion with myself. I was pretty sure that I had fallen to the left of the path, so I told myself. I began to slowly move to my right.

Very carefully I put one feet in front of the other, holding on to my bicycle for dear life. No terra firma, but just then a shimmer of light glistened through the darkness. I recognized the presence of my guardian angel who a couple of years before had given me new courage, almost new life, with a couple of moonrays.

There is a verse in Psalm 121 where the poet sings of God's protection, and he writes: "The sun will not harm you by day, nor the moon by night." Not only did the moon not hurt me but twice the moon came to my rescue.

I found the bicycle path. It was much further away than I had thought. I jumped on my bicycle and continued my travel through the night.

John 1: 4

I wonder where in our lives we could ever experience real absolute darkness. Somehow there's always at least a glimmer of light around us. It might be the silver ray of an upcoming moon, a small stripe of white under the bedroom door, or the yellowish gleam of a far away streetlight. There's always some light. Especially around the season of Christmas there is light more than at any other time. We light up our houses and put tiny lights in the Christmas trees.

On a couple of occasions in my life I have experienced total darkness. I will not bore you with descriptions of when and where, but let me tell you darkness is scary. It robs you of sight. It is like the deadly grip of an attacker. It steals away your orientation and it makes you wonder where you are.

Someone close to me is blind and sometimes I want to have a sense of what that is like. I close my eyes and wander around without sight and without failing I hurt myself colliding with some piece of furniture or a wall that all of a suddenly arises in my way.

Darkness does that to you. It strips you of certainty and it surrounds you with hazard and peril. It wraps around you like the suffocating embrace of a boa constrictor. Darkness does all that.

And as the Bible traces our beginning and totally rewinds the history of humanity and the environment to its very earliest moment all you find is darkness. There was darkness over the surface of the deep. Formlessness and emptiness wrapped in darkness. That was in the beginning so says Genesis. That's all there was.

And in that empty darkness sounded the word of God like the command of a general that sets a whole army into motion. Let there be light and there was light. Perhaps the power, the might of God is nowhere so vividly, so dramatically displayed in the Bible as there in those first sentences. Let there be light and there was light. And God saw that the light was good.

From there on in light in the Bible is the symbol for goodness, righteousness, and honesty and justice. God himself called the light good.

It is obvious that John here at the onset of his Gospel recalls that all-powerful act of God when he created light He starts his Gospel with the same phrase: in the beginning. Reading between the lines you hear John say: here is another beginning, here is a new beginning. And watch again there is the good light. John refers there to Jesus who also called himself the Light of the world. A light in the darkness. The light shines in the darkness, says Isaiah.

Let us see together first of all that with and in the coming of Jesus God made a new beginning. We can imagine the setting there in Bethlehem. Two rather youngish people, an innkeeper and shepherds. It all sort of sounds like an ordinary story in an ordinary place with ordinary people playing their role. But there is a momentous something happening there. Through the every day, ordinary circumstances, woven into the tapestry of every day life God is making a new beginning. Reconciling the world to himself.

I read a story about a couple that some forty or fifty years ago separated and divorced after two months of marriage. The man never gave up, kept having contact with his ex-wife telling her all those years that he still loved her and guess what after that long separation

45

they were re-married.

It does not even begin to compare with God's new beginning, but it is albeit vaguely, almost obscurely, a likeness of what happened there in Bethlehem. God repeats his first creative command: let there be light.

It spoke volumes to me. God did not forsake his creation. Let us personalize that God did not forsake you and God did not forsake me.

Another saying of John immediately came to mind God so loved the world that he gave his one and only son. Again I ask you to apply that to yourself God so loved me that he gave his only begotten son.

But notice also that God makes new beginnings. I once spoke to someone in one of our prisons. This man said to me that God had given up on him because of all the terrible things he had done.

But let's get this clear God did not give up on his creation and God never gives up on people. There is a prayer at the ending of Psalm 138. This is what David prays: "Do not abandon the works of your hand."

One more thought about that. There have been a few situations in my life when I could not see beyond the present. Where the future seemed closed and the end seemed near. God's own people in exile in Babylon where in that state of mind. We are stuck here in this foreign land with no hope of ever seeing the promised land again. We will never see Jerusalem again. There is no more future for us and then God's mouthpiece Isaiah comes with this wonderful message: I am the Lord that is my name, see the former things have taken place and new things I declare. With God you are never stuck in whatever circumstance. And way at the end of that wonderful book of the Bible God says to his people you will be called by a new name.

Not for nothing does the spirit through Paul call God the God of hope. God always has new things in store. So those are our first observations about the beginning of John's Gospel.

Then John continues: "The life was the light of men." I take it that the life of Jesus is a guiding light. There is that old simple question that people sometimes ask themselves when they face some problem: what would Jesus do? I think it is still a good question. And I am every time again amazed about the answer when in certain situations I myself asked that question. What would Jesus do or say. I am pretty sure that that is what Paul meant when he wrote to the Ephesians: "Live as children of light."

The Bible itself records how the answer to that question can surprise you. Let us recall just one example. The woman caught in adultery. Perhaps not written in some older manuscripts, but nevertheless accepted as trustworthy by the church.

A well-known story. Adultery was a capital offence. The death penalty was called for. All easy and straight forward: guilty and deserving of death by stoning. No doubt about it.

And what did Jesus do? You all know it. Not what all those men gathered there had expected. And Jesus promised his disciples and us all that the Holy Spirit would make it possible to find the answer to our wondering about what Jesus would do or say. This is his promise: "The counselor, the Holy Spirit whom the father will send to you in my name will teach you all things and will remind you of everything.I have said to you."

There was a time of great turmoil in the church. The question was: should Gentiles be included in the membership It came to a head when Peter had gone to Cornelius' house and even baptized him. Him being a Gentile. Great consternation and criticism all around. Not a situation that is rare occurrence in the church. Peter is called on the carpet. What is the matter with you. You enter into a Gentile's house and to make even worse you baptize him? Have you gone out of your mind? You an apostle.

And then there is that answer of Peter recorded in Acts 9 verse 16: "I remembered what the Lord had said." See how the light, how Jesus can and will shed light in the confusion that often blocks our decision making.

There is one more observation that we should not miss. That verse five: "The light shines in the darkness but the darkness has not understood it."

You note that there is that little letter a at the end of that verse. It means look at the footnote. And what does the footnote say? It says another perfect translation is: the darkness has not overcome it.

Many versions prefer that translation. And it touches my heart. I remembered that horrible scene in Gethsemane: Jesus arrested. The hour of darkness Jesus called it. Certainly there was lack of understanding. The temple police and the religious establishment did not understand did not want to understand that Jesus was the long-expected messiah. No the darkness did not understand and it looked like the end had come. But the darkness did not triumph.

That Gethsemane hour of darkness repeats itself in history. In every age again you meet it. The hour of darkness. Trace the story of humanity and you see darkness. The concentration camps of the earlier century are just one occurrence in a long trail of evil and death.

I came back from a memorial service in which we remembered those of my division killed in battle. The earth is covered with war cemeteries. Endless rows of crosses. The earth is stained with the blood that darkness caused to flow. The current cruelties of warfare are like a chapter in a never-ending book.

Certainly at the bottom of it is not understanding, not wanting to follow God's will. Yes the darkness does not understand the light. But you know what the: darkness will not conquer it either.

Through all the pitch black darkness of our time and our history shines the light that will not be extinguished. And in the end the light will totally swallow up the darkness and swords be beaten into plow shares and the prince of peace will reign.

Until that time remember what Paul wrote to the Ephesians: "Live then as children of the light."

CHAPTER SEVEN
LOST AT SEA

The moon shoots streaks of silvery light across the water. The ship's engines drone their monotonous melody. Waves splash at the bow, glittering white foam against the dark hull of the ship. The sea is calm and there is hardly a breeze across the deck.

I hear music coming from the mid-ship salon. Important government officials have their cabins there. We are billeted way down in the ship's hold. Four bunks on top of each other. Soldiers piled up like books on a shelf. There's always a stench of vomit down there. During a storm in the Mediterranean many of the men got seasick.

There are not that many of us. I don't know exactly how many, but there are ten men in my group. We're sailing across the Indian Ocean on our way to Indonesia where we are to prepare for the arrival of the battalion.

I sit on a pile of rope taking in the sight of the moonlit night and the shimmering spattering of water. It is difficult to find a place where you can be by yourself. The Klipfontein is a small ship of less than ten thousand tonnes. There are people everywhere.

As I sit there staring across the waves I discern, as if it were a brand new discovery, the vastness of the ocean. There is no shore in sight. Water all around as far as I can see. The ship's bow splits through the sea, slightly dipping and rising in ever the same seemingly endless rhythm. I begin to sense a deep loneliness within me. It is as if I am the only person in the immensity of the sea. A solitary individual floating aimlessly on the waves.

The sensation does not cause panic, but it does feel as if I am lost and there is no chance of finding the way back. I am neither home nor away. Suspended between the past and the future. The moment becomes blurred by a strange disorienting confusion. Time dissolved into emptiness.

I don't know how long the moment lasts. I hear a familiar tune coming from the salon. It is as a call to quit day dreaming.

A beckoning to enter place and time again. I make a last walk around the deck before I go down to the hold. Most men are already sleeping. I lie down on my bunk. Before I sleep I wonder how many miles I am away from where I belong. And sometimes I don't know where that is.

Exodus 25: 10-14
Numbers 9: 15-23
II Samuel 7: 5-7
Galatians 2: 20 & 21

There never was and there still is not a lot of symbolism in the liturgies of the reformed churches. Yes there are the two sacraments, perhaps a candle here and there, the cross and some other symbolic objects. Generally though there is a reliance on the spoken word. Reformed liturgies are filled with verbal expressions. There is a lot for the brain, little for the eyes and sometimes not much for the heart.

It was different for ancient Israel. People who barely escaped extinction in Egypt. No scholars among them that we know. And they did not carry a library with them on their 40-year journey through the desert. They were committed to the science of survival which for them meant the gathering of food and drink, and warding off enemies. Yet, somehow mysteriously, God chose these people to be a channel of his grace. They were to be taught about the God of heaven and earth, the God of their fathers. The lessons, however, were not offered in academic fashion for they would not understand. No catechism books, no course called Religion 101, and no seminars.

And yet they were infused with knowledge. But it is done with symbolism. Symbols were God's teaching tools. These ancient people of God were even taught the most mysterious, the hardest to understand attribute of God: the mystery of God's presence everywhere. God's omnipresence. They were to make a chest, a box of acacia wood, overlay the wood with gold, and carve poles from the same kind of wood, also plated with gold. Those poles were to be inserted into rings on the sides of the box.

Think with me about what that said to those people: poles on the ark! Exodus 25 and other passages in the Bible explain that the ark symbolized God's presence among them. Imagine the beauty of the ark; plated with gold, beautifully carved angels on top. One would say it belongs in a museum. It deserves a permanent place. It must be carefully installed somewhere. It must not be moved. Yet the poles on the ark say the opposite. The ark must not stay in one place, that's what the poles say.

Those poles on the ark spell it out: wherever you go, God goes with you. The poles on the ark symbolize and communicate perhaps even better than any learned book: wherever the journey will take you, God will go with you.

Many years ago a memorial service was held at the site of a very infamous concentration camp. The name of the camp was Treblinka. Thousands and thousand of Jewish people died there. One of the participants in the service was a survivor of that camp. His name was Samuel Wallenberg. Samuel, an old man at that time, poured out the bitterness of an almost insufferable flash-back when he said: "God was not at Treblinka." When I read it it moved me deeply. Some pain cannot be soothed with words, some wounds cannot be healed with human comfort and for some scars there is no cure.

Yet those poles on the ark tell me in spite of what anyone might think, God was there. The suffering of his people did not escape God. Isaiah was allowed to say it: "In all their distress he too was distressed." The poles on the ark tell the story of God's presence.

King David knew it: "If I go to the heavens you are there, if I make my bed in Sheol you are there, if I rise on the wings of the dawn and settle on the far side of the sea even there your right hand will hold me." And, "Even if I walk through the valley of the deep shadows you will be there."

Let's draw that to our own conclusion: if I lie in the intensive care unit with tubes sticking out of my body and doctors standing around with solemn faces, you are there. If the door of a cell clangs shut with that awfully decisive and intimidating sound, you are there. If the bottom drops out of life through whatever circumstance, you are there. For that lesson of the poles on the ark and David's song of God's presence is affirmed in Jesus Christ: "I will be with you even to the end of the age."

There is another symbolic lesson spoken by those poles on the ark: life is a journey. Especially one particular Exodus passage comes to mind. Exodus 15. The people of God had arrived at the wonderful oasis Elim. There were twelve springs and seventy palm trees. A wonderful place is was. A place where you would want to settle down. You would want to live there. But no, the poles had to be inserted again into the ark and back they went into the desert. And it was, as we noticed in an earlier chapter, back in the desert that they saw and experienced the glory of God. In the journey of life it is often in the pain of the wilderness that we become receptive to the glory of God.

The poles on the ark were also there because the ark itself could not be touched. That must have meant don't come to close. Don't get too chummy with God. Don't act as if God is your neighbour in the next tent. A certain reverend distance must be kept. Don't come too close. There was the man Uzzah who with the best of intentions took hold of the ark to keep it from falling. He reached out to support it. II Samuel 6: "Uzzah reached out and took hold of the ark of God because the oxen stumbled, but the Lord's anger burnt against Uzzah because of his irreverent act and he died." The poles on the ark also are a warning: don't come too close. Keep the sense of awe in your worship and in your talking to and about God.

Following the story of the ark in the Bible we find that after some time the ark became inert. It found a resting place in that magnificent and imposing structure that Solomon built. There the ark came to rest without being moved again. And the poles were no longer necessary. But trace that story of the ark's journey to the temple and you will find that God was not so approving of that temple idea.

Hear God's less than enthusiastic opinion in II Samuel 7 starting at verse 4: "The word of the Lord came to Nathan saying: go tell my servant David this is what the Lord says—are you the one to build me a house to dwell in? I have not dwelt in a house from the day I brought the Israelites up from Egypt to this day. I have been moving from place to place with a tent as my dwelling. Wherever I have moved with all the Israelites did I ever says to any of their rulers whom I commanded to shepherd my people Israel: why have you not built me a house of cedar?"

Listening to those words we do not get the impression that a temple was God's first choice. On the contrary, God's preference seemed to be a moveable ark. Reading carefully it becomes clear that this temple project was David's idea and not God's choice. When the structure was completed by Solomon—I Kings 6: 11—the word of the Lord came to Solomon "As for this temple the temple you are building." Notice the 'you'. Solomon must have sensed a certain tone in those words for at the dedication he said: "Will God really dwell on earth? The heavens even the highest heavens cannot contain you how much less this temple I have built."

There is one last lesson to be noticed when considering the story of the poles on the ark. It is a lesson from the New Testament People still carry God!

A missionary told the story that at one time she was on her way to a worship service in some village in South America. She arrived too late. It was already dark. She approached the village from some higher terrain. And as she looked down she saw the light in the place where the service was held, and she heard the singing of the hymn of conclusion. And then the villagers went on their way home each carrying his or her own light. The one light of the service had multiplied and it went in many directions.

It is an illustration, she said, of how the people carry God. God is not the God of Jerusalem's magnificent temple. He is not the God of anyone's private and local interest, he is the God who in that mysterious language of the Bible dwells in the heart of his people.

Where they go, he goes. Jesus Christ will be ever faithful to his promise of his presence: "I will be with you even to the end of the age."

The ancient Israelites had to carry the ark, the symbol of God's presence. In and with the presence of the ark they knew God is with us. As we ponder the poles of the ark there is still that same message: God is with us and we carry his presence. "Christ lives in me," wrote Paul, who did his share of traveling all around the Mediterranean.

As we travel life's journey it is likely that we will have to carry many burdens. Some light, some heavy, but on that pilgrimage we carry within ourselves the presence of God. That presence will always be there. It can be hidden underneath all kind of other things so that in our contact with people God's presence within us is not visible. When that happens people will see us, but not God within us.

So in the end of our pondering the poles on the ark we must remind ourselves that Christ dwells in our hearts by grace and that he must not be hidden.

Like the ancient Israelites we still carry God.

CHAPTER EIGHT
A NIGHT OF FRIGHT

I remember how the angels greeted the shepherds: "Do not be afraid." I know why those words reverberate in my mind. I am scared. Scared as if I was facing a firing squad. Scared as if were teetering on the ledge on the thirtieth floor of some building. Fear has settled into every fibre of my being. Fear in every nerve and in every muscle. My eyes survey the surroundings. It is so dark that I can see but a little distance ahead of me. I feel very exposed. I don't know whether that movement there is a branch of a banana tree fluttering in the breeze, or someone creeping in on me. I keep my rifle aimed in that general direction.

"Be not afraid." Yes but those angels were the messengers of good news. This ain't any field around Bethlehem and what's in front of me, if there is anybody there, is certainly not bringing any good news. A hand grenade would be more likely. In my mind I repeat the angels' greeting. Be not afraid. A sort of pep talk to myself. A mantra to quiet my nerves. Be not afraid.

I have only a vague idea where I am. At my back is an empty tea factory where the company is billeted. It is fairly high up a mountain. The factory is in the middle of a plantation where tea is grown. I pulled the twelve to four watch. My first time on night watch.

The sergeant said he would come by every hour or so but he has not been here yet, and I am sure more than an hour has passed since I let myself in this foxhole.

Fireflies burn little holes of light in the blackness. I know that I am not supposed to shoot at them. Our first night here the guys on watch kept firing their rifles at them. We all had to get out and man our assigned posts. It happened three or four times during that first night. I tell myself that no attending enemy would be stupid enough to crawl forward with a burning cigarette in his mouth. Still those miniature glowing lights form an eerie sight. Spooky!

I am standing in half a foot of water. I wish the foxhole would be a littler deeper. One of those short guys must have dug it. About three hundred feet to my right is another sentry. I cannot see him but I know that he sits in a rusted old automobile that has been dug in. He has a machinegun that sticks out where the front window of the car used to be. The darkness makes him invisible and I cannot call out to him. He has a more comfortable place than I. The front seat is still in the car, and he is not as exposed as I am.

Psst Carl. It comes from behind me. It is the sergeant. He is supposed to whisper the password, but he just softly mentions my name. I admire his apparently careless approach. He walks erect as if he were strolling in some park. He is an older person. Almost fatherlike to us. A veteran of the Dutch 'Prinsess Irene Brigade' which fought its way from France to the Netherlands. "Seen anything?" he asks in a half whispered tone. "No," I answer, not truthfully, for I have wondered about a lot of movements ahead of me. He tells me that it is two o'clock. Two more hours to go. I'll be back," he says not even whispering anymore, and off he goes.

His visit calms my fears. Somewhat. It is still very dark out there. But his obvious lack of apprehension rubbed off on me like sometimes a smile of another person can change your mood. My rifle is still pointed ahead, but I am not aiming it anymore.

Isaiah 9: 1-7
II Corinthians 5: 16-21

We all remember the words of Luke 2. We memorized them in Sunday school: "Suddenly a great company of heavenly host appeared saying: Glory to God in the highest and on earth peace to men." On earth peace. Yet not too long after that a detachment of

Herod's soldiers appeared in Bethlehem to destroy the peace by killing all boys under two years of age in Bethlehem.

Peace does not seem to last all that long. It is well known that during World War one on a Christmas day, soldiers from both warring sides left their trenches and in a moment of brotherhood even exchanged gifts and sang together. Shortly thereafter they again aimed their mortars at each other's fortifications.

In Hiroshima, the place burned to a crisp by the first atom bomb there is a museum called Peace Memorial Museum. What peace does it refer to there where thousands of people were simply incinerated? And where is that peace the angels announced, and was there truly peace when those soldiers left their trenches for a few hours only to resume shooting at each other a few hours later. What is peace anyway?

Once when I said goodbye to a good friend, a rabbi who was dying, he wished me shalom. He said: "Carl, shalom is all that is good in your life." And I think that pretty well defines peace too: all that is good in your life.

And when Isaiah says that the son given to us will be called the Prince of Peace I think first of all about the greatest good in life: the fact that God was reconciling the world to himself in Christ. Christ, Prince of Peace the great peacemaker. God reconciled to us and to the whole world. That announcement, I always think, is as it were tucked far away in that second epistle to the Corinthians. It is as if the announcement of a once-and-for-all cure for cancer was written up in a little local advertising paper of some hick town. Those Corinthians were with that epistle the first recipients of some truly crucial and major news.

That fact that God reconciled himself to us and to the world, as the apostle writes to the Corinthians, is such a momentous event, a happening of such earth-shattering significance that you would expect it to be written in capital letters on the first page of the Bible. God and you are reconciled. God and the world are reconciled.

Well it isn't announced with six inch fat headlines, but it is part and parcel of the whole Bible. It weaves through all its pages. Who knows how much Isaiah realized it, understood or only sensed it when he said that the son given to us would be called Prince of Peace.

There is a personal address in that title Prince of Peace. God reconciled us to himself. Us, that includes you, and me. God is reconciled with me and with you. In my pastoral career I have seen some spectacular reconciliations. I think about this husband and wife at the verge of a very bitter divorce. They spent a lot of hours in my study. They talked first to each other through me. And as the conversations wore on to many evenings, I tried to get myself out of the picture. I actually physically moved my chair way back to the wall, and yes they began to talk directly to each other. Soon after that happened I felt like an intruder on holy ground and I asked that they would talk to each other in my absence. I don't know what all was said, I do know that forgiveness took place, that pain subsided and that hostilities were ceased. A couple of years ago I was invited to their wedding anniversary. They were a very happy couple.

Something like that happened, Paul writes, between God and us. You and God are reconciled. There is forgiveness, no more pain and the enmity has ceased. You and God a happy couple.

Did Isaiah with his prophecy have premonitions of married couples reconciling? I don't think so. What Isaiah longed for and saw in prophetic fashion is the cessation of war in his time and in his country. We know the conditions of his time. The countryside ravaged by marauding armies, the cities besieged and plundered, the people in terrror.

In that war-torn time Isaiah saw, however dimly, something of God's plan for peace. The son given to us will be called Prince of Peace. Maybe Isaiah saw no further than a child born and a son given who would give peace to Jerusalem and to Judah but the angels in the fields of Bethlehem take up Isaiah's prophecy and give it its true dimension: on earth peace.

But the echo of that Bethlehem ode to peace is distorted by many dissonances. The announcement of the angels is almost drowned out by the continuing explosions of ever more deadly kinds of bombs, and the just as deadly sniping of adversaries.

And even if you are out of the reach of falling bombs or exploding grenades and you live in peace with everyone, there is no guarantee of happiness, peace or in my friend's words total goodness. There is the other rabbi of fame Harold Kushner who wrote that bestseller book "When bad things happen to Good People." He wrote another book titled: "When all you ever wanted isn't enough." In that book he writes about people in search for meaning and he uses the writer of Ecclesiastes as an example. That man had great wealth, wisdom and all kinds of pleasure, but he called it all meaningless and vanity. The peace of goodness eluded him.

Jesus' name Prince of Peace given to him by Isaiah speaks to me very profoundly on that personal level of which Kushner writes.

There are many events, many things, that can and often do disturb our peace. The wind that made the grain wave gently yesterday, blows down the trees tomorrow. So it is with peace, it can evaporate like the damp of boiling water. Relationships broken, ideals unfulfilled, hopes squashed, health gone or money missing.

Life is that way. Religious conflicts occur even between people of one family. Jesus speaks about that in Matthew 10 where he is recorded as saying: "I have not come to bring peace to the earth. I did not come to bring peace but a sword." It is one of those sayings that needs the context of the passage to gain understanding. What Jesus is saying is that religion can bring strife even in families. I have experienced that in my own family when a church schism pitched brothers and sisters against each other.

Is it possible then in this life to enjoy the peace of complete goodness? It must be for the apostle Paul speaks about the peace of God which transcends all understanding. Peace in the midst of trouble and hardship. Lewis Smedes wrote about it. The title of that little book is: "How can it be all right when everything is all wrong."

Trust me it can, trust Lewis Smedes who testifies to it, but above all trust the Prince of Peace whose promise is peace.

In order to come to peace there are all kinds of ways and means advertised. There is transcendental meditation, there is yoga, there is psycho-therapy, there are books "I'm O.K. you're O.K," and all of them might be helpful, but in the end it is what the apostle calls a fruit of the spirit.

What that comes down to is that peace is a gift. A gift from the prince of peace which he promised to his followers: "Peace I leave with you, my peace I give you." Peace, is something you pray for, it is a gift.

And I have seen it. Simple working people who would not know yoga from green apples and who would lack the time to do transcendental meditation if they knew what it was, but people who in the midst of ill fortune, and even in the deep valley of the shadow of death exuded the gift of peace. Isaiah's name Prince of Peace is a promise. Peace I leave you, my peace I give you. I pass that promise on to you and to myself this morning. The heavenly host of Bethlehem did not only address the shepherds, they still speak to you and to me about peace on earth.

But there is in that title not only a promise there is also a call. A call to be partner with the Prince of Peace. Peace is a talent to be worked with. You cannot bury it in your own heart as a private purely personal inner reality.

The Prince of Peace needs co-labourers. Peacemakers—and he has a special blessing for them, they shall be called children of God. This world needs peacemakers.

It is not an easy task, the great peacemaker, the Prince of Peace wound up on a cross. But mysteriously then and there in him the Prince of Peace God reconciled himself to us to you and to me and to the world.

In the midst of all the Christmas celebrations, with which this text is often connected, in the songs, in the lights, in the worship services, in the praise of the heavenly host please hear also the call to join the Prince of Peace.

Lastly now when the guns are not yet silenced, when police officers are shot in the streets of cities, when divorce courts work at maximum pace and people riot in the streets, now more than ever know again and do not doubt it that in the end Peace will rule among the nations, and among people, for the Prince of Peace will establish and uphold justice and righteousness.

The world, the city do not look like it yet, and it is not so difficult to lose hope as many did in the time of the apostle Peter. "Ever since our fathers died they said everything goes on as it has since the beginning of creation."

We understand their doubts, indeed ever since Cain killed Abel things have only gotten worse, Peter in answering the despair of the people of his time referred to the word of God by which the heavens and the earth were formed.

Let us also hear the word of the Lord: "They will beat their swords into plowshares and their spears into pruninghooks. Nation will not take up sword against nation nor will they train for war anymore."

CHAPTER NINE
WE ARE ALL BEGGARS
(Martin Luther)

One scout, three guys with the Brenn machine gun, two fellows with the mortar and four rifle men. Everybody carrying clips for the Brenn or grenades for the mortar. We wore cargo pants long before cargo pants became fashionable.

This is about Jan who was the fellow in charge of our mortar. He landed that job because he could not hit the side of that proverbial barn with a rifle. Somebody must have thought that there was not much precision required in mortal fire.

Jan was a religious man, although one would never tell from the vocabulary that Jan applied to life's experiences. Foul mouthed would still be an inadequate description of Jan's language. His curses were truly loathsome linguistic inventions lavishly embellished with adjectives that were no less offensive.

In addition to his many vain uses of the Lord's name, Jan committed sins that were in that time commonly defined by the word carnal. Jan always carried a little notebook around in which from time to time he would scribble notes. The notes comprised a sort of record of sins he committed. Once when Jan was a bit inebriated, not a rare occurrence, he showed me his book. It looked like the cipher code of a spy. There were crosses, slashes, plus-signs, circles and some other symbols. All of them represented one or another sinful act.

The Roman Catholic chaplain would visit our company about once every three months. He would hear confessions and celebrate mass. There was of course no confession booth. The chaplain would receive the penitent believers somewhere out of sight from the rest of us. I know that Jan took his little notebook along to confession.

Jan kept a record of his sins, and he would become restless and worried when the chaplain would not appear within the three-month cycle.

Jan's record of his sins certainly showed offences more obvious and base than those of an average person. But different than many of us, John's chronicle of trespasses had only a three month lifespan. Absolution restored him to peace and joy. He would quickly revert to his usual lifestyle, but that is another story.

Fact is that Jan needed and could accept God's forgiveness wholeheartedly and with great ease. He would celebrate his absolution with admittedly a short period of a quiet conscience.

Perhaps in spite of all his wrongdoings and improprieties, in spite of his despicable living, in spite of all his sins, Jan can still teach me the lesson that most of us need to learn again and again, namely that God does not keep a record of our transgressions. Not even for three months!

LUKE 7: 36-50

A mean person this Simon is. He invites Jesus to have dinner. That is nice of him, you think. But then he totally neglects all the customs of courtesy. No welcome kiss or hug, and no washing of the feet. So what ought we to make of this invitation? I have an idea that it is a sort of fact-finding effort. Simon wanted to have some information: who is this Jesus? What kind of a teacher is he? Is he perhaps a prophet?

So let's see what makes him tick? Invite him for dinner, but let's not overdo it. After all he is not moving in my circles and he should not get any uppity ideas. Keep him in his place, and don't use the best china. All we know about him so far is that he is a carpenter's son. Some ordinary Joe from Nazareth. Let's tone down the hospitality a notch. And so Jesus does not get the four-star treatment. Just a meal, not too elaborate and that's it.

But something happens that in Simon's opinion makes a further inquisitive conversation superfluous. No need to spend more time in talking with Jesus. Simon makes up his mind in a flash. Whatever this Jesus is, he certainly cannot be a prophet. Not only is he no prophet, but on top of that he has no manners. Letting himself be touched by this woman in my sight.

At this point I must make a confession. I must confess my cynicism. I tend to be a cynical sceptical person especially when it comes to watching the likes of Simon. Maybe it is just my age, or my many visits to the prisons of our province that have made me the opposite of gullible. Like our neighbours to the South say: I am from Missouri. So reading the passage a couple of times, a dark suspicion settled in my mind. What was that woman doing there? She was there already before Jesus came. From the time I entered she has not stopped kissing my feet. She was there. I know that there is another reading which says from the time she entered, but I read it the way it stands here. She was there. Others say that the houses were so constructed that anyone could enter at will. Might be, but that question keeps hanging around in my mind: what was she doing there?

Whatever, she had learned that Jesus was among the quests at Simon, and she does all the things that Simon failed to do. She honours Jesus. She wets his feet with her tears, and wipes them with her hair. She weeps. Those tears speak volumes don't they? Her tears are a flood of misery. A downpour of pain. In her tears the agony of wasted years, The anguish of a life of grief.

The likes of Simon would drag a woman before a rabbi, say three time I divorce you and then kick her out of the house and on to the street without any provisions for her livelihood. Of course nobody knows exactly what drove this woman to becoming what she was, a fact is she is here with Jesus weeping.

See that no words are spoken. There is nothing but the sobbing of the woman. Her tears flow freely. It is not your usual confession ritual: father I have sinned. Her tears speak louder than any words could have articulated her pain and agony. And Jesus does not ask for a verbal statement or a written testimony. Jesus sees our tears.

In Psalm 56 David gives voice to his sorrow but words fail to describe his pain and then he prays: list my tears on your scroll. God listens to tears. Interprets them. No words needed.

See her tears, hear in her sobbing a cry for mercy and compassion. Lord be merciful to me in tears and sobbing. Standing there would you not be moved to tears? Dry her tears and perhaps cradle her in your arms? Stroke her hair and make soothing noises?

Not Simon I tell you. No compassion, no pity. Just a cold conclusion: this man cannot be a prophet for otherwise he would have known that the woman who is touching him is a sinner. You can almost see his lips curl up in contempt. What a pair he thinks; a man from a no name town, and a woman who is a prostitute.

But there is one who tastes the misery of the tears, one who touches the pain of her life, one who sees her tortured days with compassion: Jesus! Let me jump ahead in the text and the passage. Verse 48: "Then Jesus said to her: Your sins are forgiven. Your faith has saved you, go in peace."

Go in peace. The words reverberated in my mind. I was once in a meeting of ministers, There was a speaker who in his lecture was commenting on a passage in this same Gospel, the Gospel of Luke Chapter 17, where Jesus says this about forgiveness: "If your brother sins rebuke him and if he repents forgive him, and if he sins against you seven times in a day and seven times comes back and says I repent; forgive him."

I remember some of the conversations around that text, and then the speaker said: "We all have this great need for forgiveness. Suppose he said, all of your life would now be shown on a screen, all your thoughts, all your words, all you ever did or thought about doing. Then—he said: and if the doors would be closed there would be a new exit in the wall so fast you would all want to leave the room."

An Anglican priest once said: yes we call ourselves miserable sinners but we mean that as a kind of religious good manners, just as we would end our letters saying: your humble servant. There is no truth in it.

And there is this little rhyme I read somewhere:

> Now I've laid me down to die
> I pray my neighbours not to pry
> too deeply into sins that I
> not only cannot here deny
> but much enjoyed as life flew by

Why was I reminded of that? It is because of Simon. It all goes by Simon and it does not touch him. She is the sinner and he is the righteous Pharisee. Nothing to do with him. And that is how we could read the passage. A sinner forgiven, a sinner restored and told to go in peace. And then sing our hallelujahs. But let me tell you we are as much involved in this episode as if we were eating Simon's offerings at his table. You, I, we cannot look at this like Simon and only make some conclusion about Jesus restoring this woman.

There is this phrase of John's epistle that aims at my life and at yours. If we say to be without sin, we deceive ourselves and the truth is not in us. Well that's where Simon is at. Maybe not exactly sinless, but then again I am only human. It's only little stuff that I could be charged with. Not worth mentioning. Certainly not something that I would lay awake about at night, and let me tell you nothing like her. No wonder she is carrying on like that. My goodness what a woman.

And then there is the word of Jesus: "Simon I have something to tell you." That's where the text forces its way into my life and into your life. Carl I have something to tell you, or Peter or Mary, There is something Jesus has to tell you.

You heard the little parable. Two men owing money. One owing five hundred denari and the other fifty, and both were broke and bankrupt with no way to repay their debt. But both saw their debt cancelled. Who will love the moneylender more, Jesus asked Simon. Of course he answered the one who had the bigger debt cancelled.

But there is something else in that little parable. I don't even know whether Simon really got it. Both men were broke unable to come up with some repayment schedule. Broke.

Did Simon get that you think? I am not so sure. Isn't Jesus saying: O.K. suppose Simon it is true as you think, you are only a minor league sinner, suppose that is true, what it comes down to is that you are in the same position as this woman. Broke. Unable to pay. No chance of satisfying the moneylender.

Simon, Johnny and Elizabeth I have something to tell you. Don't ever climb on your high horse saying look at him, look at her she is a bigger sinner than I am and what he pulled off does not even compare to my little peccadillos.

Jesus tells Simon that little five line story, but that short parable is the great equalizer that puts us all in the same position. Unable to pay the bill. But there he stands. In him the woman finds forgiveness and peace. Your sins are forgiven, your faith has saved you go home in peace.

CHAPTER TEN
BURIED TWICE

I don't know how we all got in. All ten of us in this Brenn carrier. We sit close together keeping our heads down. The roaring of the engine makes any conversation impossible. What would we say to each other anyway? It is a dangerous piece of road. Snipers somewhere up the hills on either side. Every so often we hear their fire, and twice now bullets did ricochet off the side of our vehicle. We press our heads against the side of the carrier, making ourselves as small as possible.

I know where I want to go. I have told the driver. There is a place not too far away from where we could control a long stretch of the road. The driver, a corporal, wasn't too pleased. Just a few days ago another carrier, driven by a friend of his, hit a mine, and we had to send out men to rescue the crew. The carrier will have to stay with us for a few days. The driver does not like that prospect.

We have about two or three miles to go. There has been no fire for at least ten minutes. On top of my voice I tell the guys to get out in a hurry when we stop. And keep down! There is a bend in the road where we will take our position.

The carrier moves at top speed and its tracks throw up dense clouds of dust. After a few moments we slow down, and come to a stop. "Out, out" I shout. Some of the guys jump over the side. Others get out from the rear. The last ones pass the grenades for the mortar and some boxes of ammo.

Just as I am about to jump, I see him sitting way in the back. I yell at him to get moving, but he remains where he is. Squatted at the floor of the carrier. He does not move and I sense that something is amiss. When I get close to him I see the little hole on the top of his helmet. It is no bigger than a penny in diameter, and it looks unbelievably insignificant. There is no trace of blood, only this little hole.

I know that he is dead. The driver helps me to drag his body out of the carrier. His body is still warm. We bury him there right beside the road, and we mark the grave with stones. One of the guys spelled his name "Gerrit" with gravel in the sand.

I mark the location of the grave on my map hoping that I am accurate. Years later I learn that he was re-buried at the war cemetery in Djakarta. I have seen a picture of his new grave.

I Kings 22

Summit in Samaria. Maximum security all around. Red carpets rolled out. Everybody, especially the two kings Ahab and Jehosphat, in full regalia. Ministers, military advisors, generals and court officials, and body guards. And of course more servants than there are books in the library.

What is it all about? Well as the wine flows freely and there are toasts of mutual admiration the purpose of the summit becomes clear: the royal majesties so beautifully and colourfully dressed in their royal robes are not just having an exchange of genteel niceties, they are planning a war.

You can listen with the ear of conjecture and hear in the background of the soothing dinner music of the harp, the roar of manned chariots mowing down whatever unlucky Joe stands in their way. Watch the purple of the royal robes and see the red of the blood that will flow so richly on the coming battlefield. See the generals plotting their strategies and never mind the casualties.

And look a little beyond this scene of royal splendor and you'll see some poor Ben-somebody who was just about to start harvesting his few acres of barley when the call to arms was delivered by the heralds of the king's palace. Pretty soon he will lie on the ground bleeding to death from his wounds and cursing his fate that makes him die before his time.

These two so royally dressed majesties are just two of the long list of warriors of history. Ever since Abel's blood flowed, the river has continued to course. Ever multiplying in volume as history marched on. The blood shed by soldiers killed in battle could turn the Nile red again. The tears of their survivors would form a mighty stream and the destruction caused by warfare of the ages is enough to shape a pile of rubble that would reach to the moon.

Ahab is trying to make an alliance with the king of Judah and indeed Jehosaphat assures Ahab of military co-operation. Verse four: "I am as you are, my people as your people, my horses as your horses." But then as if he is afraid of the commitment he just made, he casts about for a bit of assurance: "First let us seek the counsel of the Lord."

Well Ahab says you want assurance. Have I got assurance for you. I have a whole bunch of prophets on my payroll. Four hundred of them and we'll make them earn their pay. Bring on the prophets.

So here comes Reverend Zedekiah leading four hundred of his prophets. They are unanimous in their recommendation: The Lord will give your royal highnesses victory. God will bless your war.

Which immediately raised a question in my mind. Will God ever bless any war? Hitler's army thought so. They confessed it on the buckles of their belts: Gott mit uns. I never believed that. There is a verse in the book of Isaiah that says that God sorrowed about the distresses of the people in exile. God whose son is called the prince of peace must sorrow over our wars.

I attended the reunion of my division. The Dutch 7-December Division. At that reunion unbeknownst to any of us the government had invited forty veterans of the Indonesian Siliwangi Division with which my batallion had fought a rather fierce battle In that fight I became one of the casualties. I know the place where it happened. When at the reunion I approached one of the men of the Indonesian army and I asked him whether he knew if anyone who was at that battle was present in the party of forty. There was indeed. I sat down with that man, we drank beer, and we remembered the fury and the fright of that battle, and we both wept. Tears of emotion but also in there tears of repentance.

Let me tell you one more experience. Quite some time ago my son accompanied me to Germany where we visited the place where I was imprisoned. After the Germans were defeated in that area the Russians used the camp to house their German prisoners of war. Those Germans suffered as much deprivation as we had suffered from them. Thousands of them died and they were buried in a mass grave. My son and I stood at the site of that grave. And a couple of feet away from us was a small wooden sign stuck in the ground with one German word on it: Vater. Some child's father among the many unknowns in that grave. I am sure that God sorrowed with that child and kept her tears in his bottle of mercy.

War, when all is said and done, must cause even the angels in heaven to weep. We too weep as we remember the flow of blood that was caused by Hitler's brutes. Yes the world was liberated from that curse, but somewhere some little child put a little sign on a pile of dirt Vater, and that sign encapsulated the human misery of all wars. And I firmly believe it was a sign of God's sorrow.

No such reservations with Zedekiah's prophets. There is no holding them back. "Go", they said, "the Lord will give it into the King's hand." And there is no dissenting vote. Zedekiah and his prophets are unanimous.

Jehosaphat, however, is not quite certain about the counsel of these civil servant prophets. He finds them all too eager to please King Ahab. So unanimous they are, and so promptly they predict victory. Jehosaphat's suspicion becomes certainty, and he realizes what is going on. These prophets eat from Ahab's table. Hired help they are.

Jehosaphat wants more certainty: "Is there not a prophet of the Lord?" Between the lines you can hear him say Ahab your prophets will tell you any thing you want. They are a bunch of hirelings.

It does not seem that Ahab was insulted. If he was he hid it and he proceeds to ridicule Micaiah, who indeed was a true prophet. Not on the payroll. This is what Ahab has to say about him: he is always negative. I hate him because he never prophesies anything good about me, but always bad. He is always negative. He never gives approval for anything I plan or do.

I suspect that Ahab thought like many people of his time that Micaiah the prophet had some power over God, and that he could get God to approve whatever Ahab was about to do. A bit like General Patton of W.W. II fame. He called the chaplain a day before some offensive action and he said to the chaplain "I need good weather tomorrow and that's an order." Ahab had similar ideas. A prophet should be able to deliver. God will do what the chaplain tells him to do.

Well anyway if Jehosaphat wants that, bring on Micaiah. The messenger who had gone to call Micaiah gave him a warning. Micaiah four hundred of your colleagues have predicted victory so you better do the same thing. Let your word agree with theirs.

But Micaiah declines: "I can tell only what the lord tells me." When I read that I thought to myself there is a word of advice for everyone whoever climbs on a church pulpit to preach: I can only tell what the Lord tells me.

Micaiah is asked the very same question that the four hundred other prophets were asked: "Shall we go to war or shall we refrain." Go ahead Micaiah answers: "Attack and be victorious." Even Ahab understood from Micaiah's tone of speaking that it was a sarcastic answer. And the king urges the prophet to give him the truth about the planned war.

The truth? Here it is: "I saw all Israel scattered on the hills like sheep without a shepherd, and the Lord said: these people have no master let each one go home in peace." And as far as your four hundred hired prophets are concerned they are a bunch of liars.

"Filled with lying spirits." And what does Micaiah get for his honesty: a slap in the face from Zedekiah. And he gets thrown in a dungeon.

That I don't like. A true prophet of the Lord winds up in a dungeon. I had expected that legions of angels would be mobilized to protect him from Ahab's wrath. Instead he gets slapped in the face and put into prison. I have all kinds of questions swirling in my head about that.

Four hundred blasphemers well fed and honoured and treated like royalty and Miaciah God's obedient servant thrown in prison. Put on a bread and water diet. Lord's Day ten of the Heidelberg Catechism says: "All things come to us not by chance but by his fatherly hand." I find it terribly difficult to recognize God's fatherly hand in Zedekiah's hand that slaps God's prophet in the face. Job had the same question the same problem. Listen to him in his despair: "Does it please you to oppress me, to spurn the works of your hands, while you smile on the schemes of the wicked?"(10:3)

Is God's face, God's hand in the violence which fills this world? Do I see God's face, God 's fatherly hand in the suffering of Micaiah the faithful prophet? Martin Luther comes to our aid. He said it: you only see God's face in Jesus Christ. Looking at the situation of this part of the Bible I see that suffering is no punishment, and that in prosperity there is not always blessing.

Perhaps the writer of that letter to the Hebrews had reference to some of my questions, our questions, when he said: "Keep your eyes fixed on Jesus." That is God's face. I wish God would have dried Micaiah's tears right then and there on the spot. He did not then, but I know he did, and I know he will. And I know that at God's time the swords shall be beaten into plow shares and there will be a farewell to arms forever.

CHAPTER ELEVEN
WOUNDED

I want to grab my tommy-gun. For some reason it is lying out there in front of me. But as I reach for it I see a piece of my finger dangling from my hand like a piece of string hanging from a frayed rag. I wonder why my hand is so red. Then there is nothing.

The guy beside me is poking me in my side. "Roll on your side," he says. But I can't. He pushes me and starts ripping on my jacket. I see that my jacket is red. All of a sudden there is nothing again.

"Keep your head down," I hear, but I don't know who is shouting. There is pain in my belly. Big pain! Big huge pain! The guy beside me is yelling for the corpsman. There's a lot of shooting. I want to tell my guys to be careful with their ammo, but the sound won't come from my mouth.

Theo, the corpsman comes crawling beside me. He sticks a needle in my behind. I hear violin music and then there is nothing again. What's going on? I am moving. Swaying. What is this, a swing? Oh I see, I am on a stretcher. There I see the corpsman again. He is beside me. I want to thank him for the needle, but just then a wave of pain rushes through my whole body. It feels like a bulldozer is running over me. A heavy weight is pressing me down. I cannot breathe anymore. Then nothing is back.

Still swaying. I am still on a stretcher. The guys are carrying me. Theo walks beside me. He is holding my hand up.

"Count to hundred," he says. I wonder why. A joke maybe. But he insists.

"Count," he shouts in my ear. I want to tell him that I am not deaf, but no sound comes out of my mouth. He keeps yelling at me to count. I want him to shut up. So I count. Somewhere by nine nothing is back.

What now? Where am I? There are fellows beside me. On stretchers. But there is one guy standing up. I think I am in a truck. But I don't seem to be able to lift my head, and the pain is back. It's not in my belly anymore, it must have travelled down into my leg. It feels like an alligator is taking a bite right out of my thigh. I yell. The guy who is upright comes by my stretcher. Needle in my rear again. No violins this time, just nothing.

It must be daytime. The sun is shining right in my face. I blink my eyes. It's not the sun I see. A lamp. The pain is not bad. As a matter of fact I think I am hungry. A nurse says: "The chaplain will be with you soon" I want to ask her for something to eat, but she's gone already. An officer kneels beside me. He asks me if am ready to meet my maker. Must be the chaplain. I tell him that I am hungry, and he prays, I think, the Lord's Prayer and then he moves on to another stretcher. He must have also prayed for an angel to come to me for there is one. White! Like all angels. She, is it a she?—makes my pain go away. I want to say thank you, but nothing took the words out of my mouth.

There is that light again. There is a whole bunch of angels now. One of them curses. "Get him out of here," he says. Swaying again I notice that we are in a long corridor. Doors open. All of a sudden I know where I am. An operating room! A needle again.

PSALM 31
JAMES 4: 13-17

He was rich. Not just ordinary rich, he was super rich. A millionaire many times over. A mansion of a house; four stall garage, and more cars than those four stalls could hold. There was a wonderful swimming pool, a barbecue big enough to fry a mid-size ox, a yacht in Florida and a plane with his own private pilot.

Fifty-nine years old he was, and there were plans to celebrate his sixtieth birthday with a big party. Everything was organized. Family from overseas were invited and hotel rooms were reserved for them. At the eve of that sixtieth birthday he came home at about ten-thirty. He had a drink, watched the news on T.V., brushed his teeth, put on his pyjamas, lay down and before his head hit the pillow he was dead.

From vital, exuberant, pulsing with life, to death in the twinkling of an eye. All the preparations for travel and celebration and all the anticipation of a festive family reunion were changed to the necessity of making arrangements for the funeral.

Stories like that could fill a whole library of books. The Bible has lots of the same kind of stories. Remember Annanias and his spouse Sapphira. They did a bit of real estate wheeling and dealing and being a member of the early communually-living Jerusalem church, they were supposed to put the money, all of it, in the common treasury. The fellowship of believers of that Jerusalem church lived that way. "They had everything in common selling their possessions and goods, they gave to anyone as he had need," the Bible says. (Acts 2:45)

Annanias and Sapphira could not bring themselves to share their possessions so completely. After all Annanias had his heart set on a small vineyard that he could retire to. It would be a sort of combination retirement home and hobby farm. Sapphira was tired of having to turn every penny around, she was tired of penny-pinching. So why not hold back a little bit of all that money for themselves.

Everybody needs a nest egg, something for a rainy day. You can almost hear them rationalizing their decision to keep a bit of the money.

But you know what happened. The ink on the bill of sale was hardly dry before they were both dead and buried. There are many such stories of sudden deaths.

But let us turn to the Bible passage at hand. James writes, as he says, to Jewish believers in the diaspora. People scattered among the nations. It is to them that the apostle writes, but we firmly believe that it is a word for everybody. A word aimed at the heart of people living today, crossing the ages by the power of the Holy Spirit.

It is a word about life. It speaks about the brevity and uncertainty of our life. Verse fourteen: "…What is your life? You are a mist that appears for a little while and then vanishes." The passage also describes life as a task. Verse seventeen: "Anyone then, who knows the good he ought to do and doesn't, sins." And thirdly we read that life is in God's hand. Verse fifteen: "…you ought to say, if it is the Lord's will, we will live and do this or that."

Life is short and uncertain. I now believe that, or let me say that differently: I now know it. When I was young those words of the text: "Life is a mist that appears for a little while and then vanishes," were just words. It did not mean anything to me. Life seemed endless, certainly not a mist. I was a cool cat with more than nine lives. Life then was like an eternity. But the Bible says it ain't so.

It is different: short and uncertain. I know that this does not make sense to young people. For them life is like the horizon, step in your boat, set off from shore and sail or motor to the West. You never get to the horizon, it is always further away always in the distance. Travel to the horizon is a journey without end. That's how I thought life was, when I was young.

But then all of a sudden a whole lot of people came to my retirement party, and you say to yourself: where did the time go? Yesterday, yes it feels like it was only yesterday, I graduated from boot camp in the army, jumping out of a truck going forty kilometres an hour with forty kilogram equipment on my back and joining a forced march of forty kilometres. Then on coming home I would go out for a night on the town. That was yesterday and now today my body is clamouring for replacement parts and the government send me cheques, and I get ten percent off on senior's day at the drugstore on the last Thursday of the month. Where has the time gone?

Life, a mist, a vapor. A morning fog dissipated by the first rays of the sun. Psalm 90: "Life like the grass of the morning, by evening it is dry and withered."

The Bible keeps telling us that. It keeps saying that the end will come a whole lot quicker than most of us expect.

James also speaks about the uncertainty of life. "You say today or tomorrow we will go to this or that city, spend a year there, carry on business and make money. Why you don't even know what will happen tomorrow. Instead you ought to say: if it is the Lord's will we will live and do this or that." Even people who never took Latin in high school or in college know this one Latin phrase: Deo volente. God willing.

When I am in Europe I always visit one war cemetery. It is my way of paying tribute to those whose life ended so early. A year or so ago my wife and I visited the Margraten cemetery where almost ten thousand American soldiers are buried. We walked among the white crosses. All neatly in a row as if they had lined up at some last command. The day of their birth and the day when they were killed in battle chiselled into the stone. Some had no name on them, and the stone read: "Known only to God." All of them young. Very young! I know, because I am a veteran myself, that none of them figured to be killed in battle. What was really striking and moved us to tears was the fact that quite a few of those soldiers had been killed during the last week, the last day even, of the war. Imagine a young fellow writing to his mother: "Ma it is almost over, get the apple pie ready. I am coming home." Then some sniper shot and he was no more. You are a mist that appears for a little while and then vanishes, James says. Life is short and uncertain.

So what about that? Life short and uncertain. A lot of people either consciously or unconsciously live the eat, drink and be merry kind of life. Get the most out of it. Live it up. Let's live the beer commercial: booze, bikinis and barbecues as much as possible. And early retirement the dream to pursue.

Sometimes people retire before they have really started living. A sort of pre-death embalment into retirement. After all it is true that life is short so why not get as much pleasure as possible. A condominium in some warm climate. A cottage at the lake, living of the nest egg and the pension cheques. Hard to beat.

But then there is the word of the Bible in the last verse of the passage in James: "Anyone then, who knows the good he ought to do and doesn't do it, sins." And James is not talking about stocks and bonds and mortgage rates. James says: there is a good we ought to do.

Even though life s short and uncertain there is a task. God wants us to put our noses to the grindstone. We are his co-labourers. God wants to work with us.

And James does not beat around the bushes about what he means by doing good. It is perhaps the book in the Bible that spells out most clearly what is meant by doing good. James already comes to that point in chapter one. He is the one who makes the connection between faith and doing good. So closely does he connect the two that Martin Luther who much rather spoke about grace, wanted the epistle of James to be removed from the Bible. James states it as succinct, as clear as possible: "Faith without works is dead."

Good works for James is doing things for other people. He is the one who issued that well-known commandment: "Be ye doers of the word." Christianity has no early retirement. Following Christ has no time off for good behaviour. Being a child of God is not a part time contract that you can finish at your pleasure. Fifty or sixty years of service in the kingdom of God does not end with a golden handshake and a silver watch. James analyzes religion to its deepest core when at the end of the chapter he says: "Religion that God our Father accepts as pure and faultless is this: to look after orphans and widows in their distress and to keep oneself from being polluted by the world."

Caring for widows and orphans and all God's children is a recession-proof task. Never a down turn in that calling. Even though life is short and uncertain God wants us to use our time on earth to express in our care His wonderful grace. Life, short though it is, is a task. And don't think that James is a wet blanket who wants to take all joy out of living. Jesus Christ was not like that. He attended many parties and festivities. We can stop and smell the roses, rest and be renewed but all that in the context of our calling.

The last observation that comes to mind considering the Bible passage is that fact that life is in God's hand. James says it this way: "You ought to say if it is the Lord's will we will live and do this or that." Our life is in God's hand. David says in Psalm 32: "My times are in your hand."

There is safety in that. Insurance. Everything of life is Deo Volente. It is all in God's hand. He is the giver of life and in His hands is the ending. He decides. Taste and touch the security in that for life in God's hand is not something that God would regard lightly. We know that our life is terribly important in God's sight for He went a long and painful road to secure it and make it everlasting.

So, we see Jesus. In him, the Son of men, we see how precious life is in God's sight. Psalm 90 puts the length of our life at seventy years. Nowadays we can stretch that a bit with open heart surgery, vitamin pills and organ transplants. But in the end it is not a whole lot. Hebrews 9:27: "Man is destined to die once." But that is not the end. What it is exactly is hard to describe and to define. The old Preacher in the Book of Ecclesiastes called it the separation of the body and the soul. Whatever it is, what we call death, it is not the discontinuation of life. For our lives are in God's hands and He won't let go of them.

This sermon started with a story. Let me end with another story. Both are true.

This last one is a story of war and blood. A young man on a stretcher. Three bullets went through him. One through his stomach which is as every soldier knows the big one. The one to hand in your number. The young man reached the field hospital where doctors first helped others who had more chance to survive. The chaplain came to this young man and told him that he was about to meet his maker and he prayed with him.

Early the next morning the doctors found this young man still alive and they operated on him, and he lived. I know for I was that young man. Not so young anymore now, but very much alive. You see our lives are in God's hands.

CHAPTER TWELVE
AT THE ARMY HOSPITAL

What is all this white stuff? Snow? It feels smooth, I glide my hand over it, and I notice that my hand too is white. I try to identify the smell around me, but I can't. It is a mixture of aromas, but somewhere in it is something I recognize. It is a hospital smell. My eyes then catch up with my nose. I look around. Yes, I am in a hospital and there is a nurse sitting beside my bed.

I haven't seen a white woman in I don't know how long. I notice that she is a very attractive looking girl. She wets my lips. She knows my name, and she asks how the pain is.

I am about to tell her that I have no pain when it hits me like a hammerblow. Pain all over. My hand especially. She stands up, and comes back with a needle. My behind must look like a pin cushion, I think. Then nothing is back.

I am in and out of somewhere where there is nothingness. But this time I wake up and I hear a voice that I have heard before. The doctor, I think. But the voice keeps calling my name. I try to focus on the person, and to my amazement I see that it is my brother. He is a Marine and he has caught a flight across the island.

He sits beside my bed., He doesn't say much, and I can only stammer. After a while he leaves. I begin to feel a bit more with it.

I look under the blanket. My right leg is all in plaster. My right hand is wrapped up and there is gauze around my stomach.

Morning, I think it is a morning. It is still dark. A chaplain, I think it is a chaplain, puts a wafer in my mouth. A eucharist wafer. I don't know what he says to me, but I appreciate the wafer.

I am hungry, and when the nurse comes again I ask for something to eat. She brings me little pieces of ice. Not really a satisfying meal, I think. When she comes back, I complain to her, and she tells me that the doctor would have to give permission for something more substantial.

The next day I get indeed more substantial stuff: ice cream and pudding with whipped cream on top. I don't know for how many days I get that diet, but I do remember the first dish of rice. Delicious!

The good looking nurse comes with a wheelchair. "I am taking you for a walk," she says. She wheels me outside, and I relish the sight of the sun and the smell of grass. There are guys walking along the paths. Some have wooden leg pegs, like I have seen in movies about pirates.

After about half an hour I am back in my bed. "Do you want something, she asks. "A beer," I say, but all I get is ice cream and a little piece of mango.

The walks become more frequent, and after some time they are an afternoon ritual. We now leave the hospital grounds once in a while. It is always the good looking nurse who wheels me around. I now know her name: Annie.

The doctor comes by every afternoon. One day he tells me that he can fix my finger." Set it straight," he says. I thank him, but I decline the offer. I have had enough pain for a while. "Coward," I say to myself.

After some time I lose my wheelchair, and I get a pair of crutches instead. I begin to hop around. I am free to go wherever I want, as long as I stay on the hospital grounds.

After six weeks or so I am transferred to a rehabilitation centre. Will I ever be rehabilitated......?

I Peter 2: 1-12
Genesis 47: 1-12
Forced by famine, Jacob once more has to make a difficult journey. Tired from travelling, exhausted from spent emotion in the reunion with his beloved Joseph, and generally worn out, he has an

audience with Egypt's ruler the Pharaoh. And when Pharaoh saw Jacob he asked: "How old are you?"

Old age must have been written in capital letters on Jacob's figure. The years chiselled lines on his face. There is, I think, a bit of amusement in Pharaoh's question: wow this is really some old man. How old are you really? The twists and turns of Jacob's turbulent life must have left him marked with age. An old man he is. Visibly so. A time-worn traveller.

Notice, however, that Jacob does not consider himself very old. My years have been few, he says. Difficult yes, but few. Strange that is. It is hard to think of yourself as old. There is that familiar expression: you're only as old as you feel. If that were true all pension funds could be discontinued for very few old people feel themselves old. Somewhere in our being we remain young and vital. I can add my personal testimony to that. In spite of my white hair, my rheumatic limbs and all the old age frailties, I feel young. It is my body, like Jacob's that betrays me. It refuses to stay young. On the contrary it begins to clamour for replacement parts.

Pharaoh looks at Jacob and sees a man stooped with age, bent with the burden of time, and filled with the thousands memories of times past. But Jacob says: "My years have been few."

In many ways the Bible agrees with him. It does say that our years are few. Psalm 90: "The length of our days is seventy years or eighty if we have the strength, yet their span is but trouble and sorrow for they quickly pass." Gone before you know it. You just begun to gather a little wisdom, you feel that you are ready to make a start with your life, and to your great amazement there is the first pension cheque in your mailbox.

The apostle Peter says it this way: "All men are like grass, and all their glory is like the flowers of the field, the grass withers and the flowers fall." Game over!

There are often these wonderful offers in my mail. Everything from soup to nuts at sharply reduced prices. Call this number now. Fill out this form now. Send your response now, immediately. Cut this coupon forthwith. All of it accompanied by the admonition: do not delay. Do it now. Do not wait. There is a similar exhortation in the Bible. A biblical do it now.

When Jacob says that his years have been few there is a biblical echo to this words. "Man born of a woman is few of days."(Job 14)

The Bible wants to warn us that our time is limited. And that ancient Preacher sums it up in Ecclesiastes at the beginning of his last chapter: "Remember your creator in the days of your youth." Do not delay. Do it now when you are still in possession of all your faculties. Remember your creator. Remember that he so loved you that he joined you in the brevity of life. Hardly more than thirty years he was with us. Remember it before the time comes when you cannot even remember what you did yesterday.

Jacob also calls life a pilgrimage. What he means to say is that he was a stranger in a foreign land. I have never reached my destination. He has reference to the fact that he lived an unsettled homeless life. Jacob had not yet come into possession of the promised land. Wherever he lived, he did not really belong. A nomad he was. A travelling foreigner.

The epistle to the Hebrews ending that long list of people who persevered in the faith says, "None of them received what had been promised." And in verse thirteen: "They only saw them and welcomed them from a distance. And they admitted that they were aliens and strangers on earth. People who say such things show that they are looking for a country of their own."

So it was with Jacob. Always on the go. Coming from somewhere and going somewhere else. All the time pitching tents. Jacob the wanderer. Then here, then there. Hardly did he settle down in Bethel or a famine occurs and off he goes again to Egypt where he reunites with his beloved son Joseph. But still and again a foreigner in a strange land.

It conjures up pictures of refugees. People away from their homeland, driven from their houses and possessions. The world is full of them. Their pictures are on our T.V. We read their stories in the paper. How different is our life. If we move we don't often move beyond the borders of our own land. We don't live like strangers in a foreign land. Wherever we go we take our credit cards along. We have our own little lots, our own condominiums and our own houses. Even if we move we are settled people, We carry our passports that show that we belong.

But wait a moment. What does Peter the apostle mean when he writes: "Dear friends I urge you as aliens and strangers in this world." Or at the beginning of his letter: "To God's elect, strangers in this world." Strangers in this world?

It really means the same for us as what Jacob wanted to say: I have not arrived yet at my destination. I am still on the way. I am a pilgrim. Yes the Bible applies that word to us even though we are people with a fixed address. People with the deed and title to our property in the safety deposit box. People with petunias and impatiens blooming in our front yard.

In spite of all that groundedness the Bible calls us pilgrims, strangers, aliens in this world. People who have not yet reached their destination. People who have not yet arrived at their homeland. People on a temporary assignment.

Genesis 47: 11 shows the mirror of our own existence. Father Jacob speaks for us all: "My years have been few, and they were the days of my pilgrimage."

Is that then a morbid thought? A wet blanket on the beauty and the wonderfulness of life? A sort of party pooper sermon? Let's all sit down and prepare for our funeral sermon? It certainly is not meant to be that. Jacob says that his pilgrimage was difficult. But that is not always the case for everyone. Life is beautiful, wonderful indeed. Glorious. And it is to be enjoyed.

But so far we have met two caveats: it is shorter than you think, therefore remember your creator in the days of your youth, and secondly life is a pilgrimage. We have not yet reached our home even when we have lived in the same house for fifty years. There is another house waiting. Our Father's house with many rooms. The apostle Paul calls it a building of God, an eternal house in heaven.

The time of life slips through your hands like sand through your fingers. When Jesus told his disciples about the house of many rooms he said first: "Let not your hearts be troubled." Those words accompany us on our pilgrimage. Let not your hearts be troubled.

As we read on in the passage we see that Jacob blessed Pharaoh. Pharaoh had just given Jacob's family grazing rights to the best land in Egypt—Goshen. But there was nothing Jacob could give in return. Jacob was a beggar. But there was one thing he could give: he blessed Pharaoh.

It reminds me of a story I read about Tolstoy. Tolstoy was walking somewhere when he met this beggar. A panhandler. And as was his custom Tolstoy reached in his pocket to give the man some coins. But his pocket was empty. He had forgotten to take his wallet. "Brother," he said to the beggar, "I cannot give you anything for I have no money on me." And the beggar answered: "You have given me the best gift ever: you have called me brother." The best of gifts are often not monetary.

I don't know what kind of blessing father Jacob passed on to the Pharaoh. The verb used implies the bending of the knee and the paying of homage. Probably what is referred to is something that happens to me once in a while when I sit down with people to eat a meal and someone will ask: Reverend will you say the blessing." I then pay homage to God the giver of all good things.

I think that's what Jacob did. He recognised the giver and he paid homage to him. No wonder you say. Look at it. Jacob and his whole family go almost in one instant from rags to riches. From famine to feast. No wonder he recognises the giver.

It is perhaps not so easy anymore for us to recognise the Great Giver. We haven't gone from rags to riches. We drive around in our automobiles, wear nice clothing, live in beautiful homes. Three square meals a day. Insurance premiums paid. We worked for it didn't we? What we got we got because we worked hard.

Yet I see in Jacob's poverty a bit of myself. In spite of all my worldly possessions there is a way in which the Bible declares me poor like Jacob arriving empty handed at the court of Pharaoh. Isn't that what the word grace implies?

"By grace you are saved and this is not from yourselves." Before

God I am like Jacob before Pharaoh. Nothing in my hand I bring. And yet like Jacob received a home so I have the assurance of the Father's house with many rooms. Like old Jacob received the best of the land, so I am the recipient of innumerable gifts. Too many to mention them all. Count you blessings one by one, we sing, but how could I? It would keep me busy from morning till evening. There would be no end to it. Were the whole realm of nature mine even that were a present far too small. There is no way I could ever pay God. I must live by grace. And Jacob shows me the way: Jacob blessed Pharaoh.

The gifts of God's grace are countless. Morning by morning new mercies await us. What rests us to do on our pilgrimage is to bless the Lord. And I do so taking the words of the apostle Paul: "Praise be to the God and Father of our Lord Jesus Christ who has blessed us in the heavenly realms with every spiritual blessing in Christ. For he chose us in him before the creation of the world to be holy and blameless in his sight. In love he predestined us to be adopted as his sons and daughters through Jesus Christ in accordance with his pleasure and will to the praise of his glorious grace which he freely bestowed on us."

Blessed be the God and Father of our Lord Jesus Christ!

CHAPTER THIRTEEN
WHERE IS HOME?

The ship has just docked at Rotterdam. It is early in the morning. Longshoremen come aboard. I am amazed how white people are. Their faces look like they are painted eggshell white. I am even more amazed that white people are lugging stuff around. I haven't seen white people do any physical labour in four years now.

We enter a hall where officers sit behind tables. When my name is called. I come forward and receive four hundred guilders. I am also assigned to a bus. I am to see to it that all the guys on my bus get home. I will be the last.

Our ship arrived about twelve hours late. The pilot could not reach us because of the stormy sea. As I deliver some of the guys at their homes I notice that at some addresses the festivities have gone on all during the night and some of the parties are quite drunk.

I see about twenty-five guys home and then finally it is my turn. The bus turns into my street. It stops in front of number ten. Later they tell me that the door was decorated. I do not see it. I see my father. As soon as I am out of the bus he embraces me. He has never done that before and never since. We are more the handshaking family.

The flat is filled with visitors. My fiancee. Neighbours. Aunts and uncles and a few girls that I have dated. How long is that ago? I get presents. A shirt with fifty cents in the pocket because the shirt my brother got on his homecoming was fifty cents more expensive.

Everybody wants to know where and how I got wounded, and how

I feel. I feel queasy. Out of place. People are so white and they talk so strangely. It is so small here. The teacup in my hand is so fragile. I feel as if I don't belong here. But this is my home, I keep telling myself. This is your family. These are your friends. Yet I am not comfortable.

I want to get out of my uniform, and I long for a bath. My mother hands me a teakettle with warm water. I don't know what it is for, but then I remember: you put the water in the basin and sponge yourself.

At night I walk my fiancee to my uncle's house where she stays. My mother will not allow her and myself under one roof. I feel even more quaint. Like some giant hand misplaced me, and I can't even find myself.

I go to sleep in my brother's room, and I have a terrible nightmare. I wake up yelling. Everybody wakes up, and my father brings me a glass of water.

As the days go on, I feel more and more unrelated to my environment. I get together with some of my guys. I don't know how we find each other. But somehow we meet in this bar in Amsterdam. I dress in my uniform again. So do the others. We talk and drink. We drink too much. My father admonishes me, and tells me to get back to work.

I think about signing up with the army. Maybe that is where I belong. But I am indecisive. I have trouble sleeping. The bed is too soft, and there is no sound at all. I am not used to silence. I sleep in in the morning. My father does not like that. He keeps talking about going back to work.

I walk a lot. I have a bit of a limp. Mostly I wind up at night in Amsterdam with the guys. One night, catching the last train home, I fall asleep and miss my stop. A custom officer wakes me up at the border. I managed to get home, but my father had locked the door. He thinks I should be home at eleven o'clock. I think about taking off to wherever. Get away from here. I manage to wake up my brother who opens the door.

I don't like the weather. It is chilly and it rains a lot. I don't understand myself. For four years I wanted to go home. Now I am home and I am not sure that this is where I want to be. At night I talk with the guys about it. They have the same feelings, and one of them has already signed up with the army for another four years. At times I am tempted to do the same thing.

I walk the familiar streets. My limp is almost gone. But the feeling of unsettledness remains. I cannot talk about it with my family. Everybody wants me to go back to work. Just go on where I left four years ago. What they don't see is that I am not the same as I was four years ago. Who am I now? I wish I knew...

EXODUS 14: 15

Talk about being caught between a rock and a hard place. This Bible verse paints the proverbial position of two no win choices. Here is the all time insoluble dilemma. The people of God camped before a sea they could not cross and the Egyptians they could not defeat at their back. The sea they could not survive or a battle they could not win.

Life sometimes makes you confront these situations. When there is no way you could move forward. Much less could you go back, and you are unable to make a move. Stuck in a hopeless pair of circumstances.

It is really no wonder that the people of Israel complain loudly and bitterly: "Was it because there were no graves in Egypt that you brought us to the desert to die? What have you done by bringing us up out of Egypt? Didn't we say to you in Egypt leave us alone, let us serve the Egyptians. It would have been better for us to serve the Egyptians than to die in the desert."

The passages from the Book of Exodus touch our lives in many ways. This particular episode of our text occurred only once. It is "einmalig" as the Germans say, but our lives too are a pilgrimage. A journey to a promised land. A journey with God we firmly believe.

Yet sometimes we too get stuck in these impossible situations where we do not know what to do next. We get caught not between the Red Sea and pursuing Egyptians, but in our own seemingly insoluble life-situations.

The writer of Psalm 77 apparently was at one time in such a state. Listen to him: "I cried out to God to hear me. When I was in distress I sought the Lord. At night I stretched our untiring hands and my soul refused to be comforted." Stuck in his grief, he was, unable to move on. On a cemetery I met this young woman whose husband had died and she too could not be comforted. She said: "My life is over."

The way of God's people is, as we all know, not always a walk on easy street. On the contrary all too often it is a via dolorosa. A journey of pain and sorrow leading to the question that echoed on Golgotha: why, why. The Israelites stuck at the shore of the Red Sea certainly does not picture the first occasion where the doors of the future seemed closed and where the present offered only anguish and suffering.

Remember Abraham's walk to Mount Moriah. The longest three day walk ever. Isaac his son, the joy of his life, the hope of the future, chatting incessantly beside him. "Father how come you did not take along a lamb for the sacrifice?" "How long yet before we are there?" "Will we build a small altar?" We can imagine the questions, and we can taste the agonizing discomfort of Father Abraham. Stuck between the choices of that moment: obedience to the God of the covenant is going to cost him his son, and saving his son will cost him his God.

And thinking beyond the Israelites at the shore of the Red Sea, thinking beyond Abraham, and who knows how many millions more caught in the terrible dillemnas of life, I see God in that agonizing seemingly inextricable choice between his love and his righteousness. The people he chose and loved forever lost all too often in the rebellion of idolatry and unfaithfulness, and God unable to forsake his love. The solution of that occurred on the Golgotha hill.

Here too in our text God acts. Moses is told: "Tell the Israelites to move on." I call it the impossible command. How could these people move on? Thousands and thousands of them, women, children and cattle, they all face the sea and there are no boats available to cross the water. So then how are they to move on?

That is exactly the question people ask when stuck in those impossible choices. These are the words we all have heard: "I don't know how I can go on." Look in the Bible passage at the impossibility of obeying that command "Tell the Israelites to move on." Impossible we respond.

Just like the people there: "It would have been better for us to stay in Egypt and die there." It is so terribly difficult to discern God's future. The darkness of the present shields our eyes of faith for the brightness of God's future.

God's future. Amazing! Incomprehensible! Tell the Israelites to move on. It is a word of God first to his people who knew themselves to be stuck at the shore of the Red Sea. Never mind that sea. Never mind the impossibility of the command. Never mind that you raise your eyebrows in doubt and that you say it cannot be done. Never mind that it makes no sense to you. This is the word of God Almighty: "MOVE ON."

Hidden in that command of times long past, in those few words of the Bible easily glanced over, see the majesty and the power of the creator. The God who beckons his people to move on into his future.

That command to move on also exposes the smallness of our faith. The protests of the Israelites jump from the page. Move on, it is a laugh you hear them say. Yes but it is really is the laugh of Sarah when she was told that she would become pregnant. In that laugh is the little faith of the disciples on the waves of the sea: "Master we are perishing."

But listen; somewhere in the laughing contempt of the Israelites, in Sarah's smile of scorn, in the disciples' cry of despair is the sight and the sound of our own lack of faith. How could that widow again find just a little bit of joy in her life? How could that marriage be saved? How could anyone live with such a handicap? How can you move on when you are stuck?

Well the Bible tells us what happened. The impossible happened. Moses stretched out his hand over the sea, and the waters divided. There was a path for God's people to cross the sea. The impossible happened.

And God does not want his people to forget this event. The Passover to be kept throughout all the following generations is to keep the memory alive. Israel's God is no longer simply God, He is, and every man, woman and child must know it, Almighty God, the God who created a path through the sea for his people.

Philips, a well-known Bible translator wrote a little book with the title: "Your God is too small." All too often that title encapsulates our own faith. We lock up God in the cages of our impossibilities. It cannot be done, we say. And we eliminate from our faith the God who made a path through the sea.

Ages after the event of our text the children of the people who stood caught in hopelessness on the shores of the Red Sea, were stuck again. Overpowered by a foreign nation, imprisoned by their enemy, and enslaved into captivity, separated from their beloved Jerusalem temple, they echo the cry of their forefathers: we are stuck. There is no way out. God, even if He wanted, cannot help us.

And then the word of God comes by them by the prophecy of Isaiah. Isaiah 43:16: "This is what the Lord says, he who made a way through the sea, a path through the mighty waters, who drew out the chariots and the horses, the army and re-enforcements together and they lay there never to rise again extinguished, snuffed out like a wick.Forget the former things do not dwell on the past see I am doing a new thing now it springs up, do you not perceive it.I am making a way in the desert."

And when the time of the return came the people of God must have said: "We confess that we had never thought of that." We moved on into the future beyond even our wildest hope and expectation.

Now let the Bible speak to you and to me. See again our faith often smaller than even the mustard seed faith. Our unwillingness to know in our heart that God can make widows sing, create a smile on our lips and a bounce in our step when we had given up.

David knew that even in the darkness of life's deepest valleys there is a God who will lead you through. This sermon ends with the words of a hymn sung already by the ancient church:

Come ye faithful raise the strain
of triumphant gladness
God has brought his Israel into joy from sadness
loosed from Pharaoh's bitter yoke
Jacob's sons and daughters
led them with unmoistened foot through the Red
Sea waters.

Dare we hope in God's wonderful future? He who embodies that future answers our question: "Do not be afraid. I am the First and the Last. I am the living one. I was dead, and behold I am alive for ever and for ever. And I hold the keys of death and Hades."

CHAPTER FOURTEEN
THE PURSUIT OF NORMALCY

I am out of my uniform now. Once in a while I am tempted to put it on again. The clothes from four years ago feel strange and they do not fit well. I myself do not fit well either. I still feel as if I am on furlough. Away from my outfit and my guys, but having to return soon to wherever we are posted. I have not had a nightmare for some time, but I have reached for my weapon under the bed a couple of times.

I have gone back to work. I am in re-training in the accounting department I feel, however, that I am being re-habilitated into civilian life. I am like a prisoner who after his release must learn the rules of good behaviour again. I am told that I cannot be without a tie. I answer that I agree and that the tie is in my pocket. The chief lady smiles with the sort of sympathetic grimace that people put on when they overlook some unruly comportment of their pet.

Together with my fiancée I visit the scout of my platoon. He lives not too far from here. He is not home. There is a mattress at the bottom of the stairs. His mother explains that he often comes home drunk. The mattress catches him when he falls down the stairs.

I have quit going to Amsterdam at nights. I am trying to become "normal." That's what my family wants me to do: be normal. I have gone back to school. A private nightschool. Some civil servant who came aboard in Port Said promised me that the Department of Defense would pay the tuition. But when I asked for the money they looked at me as if I was from a different planet. I pay myself which leaves me little pocket money. I aim to get my High School diploma in two years.

I still feel lonely. It is as if I am not connected to myself or to others. I have lost the key, but I don't know to which door. I am lost. Lost in my hometown where I know every street and corner, lost in my own family, lost in myself.

I go to church and hear about hell. I go to the office and hear about parties. I come home and I hear that I am still not settled.

Sometimes on Sunday mornings when I walk with my fiancee in the dunes I hear the birds sing. It's the only sound that cheers me up somewhat. I love to walk there and hear the waves hit the beach.

I buy a second-hand bicycle. I ride to the office in the morning. It rains often, and I pedal through watery streets. I walk around for the rest of the day with wet pants. Not only are they wet, they also stink. The scent of wet wool clings to me. Is that going to be my life, I wonder. Bicycling to the office in wet pants five out of six mornings. My father has done that all his life. It has soured him. We do not have much in common. We don't talk, except on Sunday afternoons when we do the crossword puzzle together. Without that puzzle we would never talk.

My mother does not pay much attention to anyone of us. She cooks and does grocery shopping and visits with the neighbours. In the afternoon she goes to movies with her friends. Even though movies are still a taboo in our circles. At night she reads or darns my father's socks. She tells me that I am doing better. When I ask her what she means, she says I am more normal.

I hate the word normal. Yet I am trying. Robert Frost would understand....

THE LOCKLESS DOOR

It went many years,
But at last came a knock,
And I thought of the door
with no lock to lock
I blew out the light,
I tip-toed the floor,
And raised both hands
In prayer to the door.
But the knock came again
My window was wide;
I climbed on the sill
And descended outside.
Back over the sill
I bade a Come in'
To whatever the knock
At the door may have been.
So at a knock
I emptied my cage
To hide in the world
And alter with age.

CHAPTER FIFTEEN
AN AUSTERE WEDDING

I tremble a bit. What is it, nervousness, or just a shiver because this bone-chilling cold rain that will not stop? It is probably a combination of the two. I am nervous, very nervous, but I am also cold. An hour or so ago the mayor of the village declared us officially and legally married. He held a ten minute speech of which already now I do not remember one single word. At the end of the ceremony there were limousines waiting for us to take us to the church.

Now we are standing in front of the church where our marriage will be blessed by the officiating clergy. He has made a long journey to this village. He is the chaplain of my battalion. I still call him my chaplain. He once visited me on a dark night in my foxhole. He reads a form and then drones a rather long question. I am supposed to answer: "Do you take Martha as your legal wife...." All the while I am thinking this rather unholy thought: "Who is paying for these cursed limousines?" I have not ordered them. I don't have money for that kind of luxury. Not only no money for luxury, no money period. I am broke. I voice my affirmative—yes—all the while worried about expenses.

My wife too sounds her "Yes" and we are asked to be seated. An all-girl choir sings. Way off tune, but their song expresses best wishes, and I know they mean that wholeheartedly. It makes it a little easier to listen, although I wish they too would sit down.

The chaplain reads scripture: John 2. The text for his sermon is rather predictable: John 2 verse 2: "Jesus had also been invited."

It is difficult for me to concentrate and hear what he is saying. I am nervous. Not only about the cost of the limousines, but also about a whole lot of other things. Both our families do not approve wholeheartedly of our marriage. My family wants me to wait till I finish university, and Martha's family deplores the rather austere ambiance of the wedding. She does not wear the traditional wedding garb. They wanted me to pay for a much grander affair which I could not afford and which again like a returning refrain raises in my mind with a soft but persistent voice the question about the cost of those limousines.

Both families do indeed have valid reservations about this marriage. True I have no money. True my education is not yet even at the half-way stage. They are right. All kinds of relatives have voiced their reticence. Some more subtly than others. I know that at least some of them think that we get married because Martha is pregnant. Which she isn't. So why do I get married? Even while the chaplain is preaching I ask myself that question. I love her, I know that. I have loved her since I saw her that first morning when she wore that crazy half-tilting green hat. But there is more than just simply love. There are many answers to my own question. It is impossible for me to stay home. My parents are wonderful people, but their curfew for a twenty-five year old veteran is ridiculous. I do not have a key to the house. There is a seething restlessness in my being which calls for changes and movement like the unceasing tides of the sea. It's hard for me to follow routine. A hardly subdued frenzy lies inside me like a secret locked in a safe. My father sees some minor benefit in my marriage: "Maybe it helps you to settle down," he says.

My wife too was not all together sure about getting married. She is a practical woman and she raised all kinds of practical questions. There is no housing available. We have no money. Our families would like us to wait. You are still working on your education. She was right. So again, why do I get married? I don't hear a word of what the chaplain is saying. And the cost of the limousines keeps popping up in my mind like a recurring theme of a tragic opera.

I do catch the phrase that the chaplain repeats a couple of times: "Jesus was also invited." A very irreverent thought floats through my mind like unwanted flotsam at a cottage shoreline: "He must have invited himself for I have not given that invitation a thought." My preference had been to elope. This wedding on the cheap is a compromise that was forced on me.

Now more than fifty years later I know that I was right. He did invite himself. He wanted to be part of our life together. And he knew that we wanted him to be present in our lives.

The chaplain says amen. The girls sing once more. A prayer, and we go out to the waiting limousines. I find out that my brother-in-law has ordered them. I also find out that I am supposed to pay for them. There goes the last of my money.

Much to the dismay of both gathered families we leave early in the evening to catch the last train. Even so we arrive when it was already morning. Two rooms and the use of the kitchen! Our honeymoon suite and our home. For some time anyway.

JOHN 2: 1-12

I stood in front of this painting. First close by then a few steps backwards. Squinting at it from close by and then from further away. I saw a rather abstract mass of dark colours. I was about to walk away from it when something compelled me to go back and look again. All the time I was asking myself what is this about? Is there any meaning to it at all or is just black darkness. Then my eye fell on this tiny streak of white that as it were rose up out of the darkness. Something dawned on me. I think I began to understand what the artist wanted to say with this painting. Not the common saying "Light at the end of the tunnel." Not that, I thought. Something else. Look long enough at the darkness, and you see how darkness gives birth to light. That tiny streak of light illumines the darkness.

That is what I thought about as I read and reread the account of the wedding at Kana. Jesus is there. A man like any other man. Nothing distinguishes him from any of the other male guests at the party. As Pontius Pilate said some years later: see the man. That's what people saw a man. Yet John thinking about the event years later says, but there was something that showed there was more than just any ordinary man. All of a sudden some event showed that there was more than a mere man. All of a sudden, unexpectedly, something dawned on us—we saw his glory. That's how John begins his gospel: "We have seen his glory." There in Kana was a moment of discovery. An epiphany. There is more to him than his visible humanity.

So let's together see what led to this epiphany. It happens at the beginning of Jesus' public ministry. On the third day, John writes. Jesus and his disciples attended this wedding feast. The party is in full swing. Speeches, toast to the bride, toast to the groom, and toast to anybody around. And then all of a sudden there is this uncle of the bride who wants to toast his sister, the mother of the bride. A short speech, he lifts his glass, and an awkward silence falls over the crowd, as if in the midst of all the festivities someone had made a very sad announcement about the death of a relative. The glass is empty, and so are the other glasses and the servants have not filled them because there was no more wine. Well what do you do? You carry on as if nothing happened of course. Let's not embarrass the family. But let's call a spade a spade for all practical purposes this party has come to an end. It was like a book from which somebody has ripped out the last chapter You come to an end before you should have. So it was with this party. Embarrassment all around. I bet somebody must have thought if not said: "Oy veh what a bunch of cheapskates."

We don't know how that really happened. One commentator says that is was Jesus' fault. He should not have brought so many disciples with him. But the text says: "Jesus and the disciples were invited." Maybe the family had invited the disiciples out of politeness because they had come with Jesus and you had to include them for the sake of hospitality Whatever. All of a sudden the party collapses like a pricked balloon. Already here and there people say in half-whispered voice: let's go home.

Then Mary speaks with her son. "Jesus they have no more wine." Hear the implied question there. Can't you do something about that.

There is no more wine. From Jesus' answer you can see that Mary's words were more than just a statement of fact. There is more than that "They have no more wine." There is an unspoken expectation my son can do something.

It is a curious exchange of words there. Mary: "They have no more wine." Jesus' answer is a bit gentrified or sanitized by the N.I.V. but literally translated he says: "What is it to me or to you, my hour has not yet come." Luther comes close: "Weib was habe ich mit dir zu schaffen?" What have I to do with you? I cannot catch or understand the undercurrent of this very brief conversation. There is that unspoken question. An assumption that Jesus can change the situation. Is Mary already convinced that Jesus has the capacity to perform miracles? Or is there even an equally unspoken accusation: it is your fault, you brought all those disciples? I think she expects Jesus to do something. Do what he tells you to do she says to the servants.

And why is Jesus' answer so sharp? Why woman instead of mother? What does it mean, my time has not come yet? Is that related to the time when he shall be arrested and crucified? Commentators have all kinds of answers to the questions. They hang a bit of theology on it. Mary the intercessor. Jesus biding his time.

I confess that I do not understand this exchange of words. Something beyond my understanding is going on there. I hear Mary's question and Jesus' answer, but I wasn't there I don't know the tone of voice, the gestures or that cross current of the conversation. But I know what happened. Jesus changes the water that was meant for ritual cleansing into wine. A lot of wine.

Now let me tell you the things I do understand. Let me first of all refer to the last verse of the passage. This is the first of his miraculous signs. There is an unusual emphasis on that word 'this'. This was the first sign. It is as if John wants to say: it says something about Jesus. This is what he did. We do that too sometimes. We ask someone "Do you know so and so?" and then in answer people will say: "Let me tell you what he did." This is what he did and that then tells you what kind of person you are talking about. I think that is John's intention.

This is the kind of man he was. He changed water into wine. He wanted the party to go on. Jesus is not someone who looks down on festivities. He is not one who takes the joy out of life. There is a Dutch book with the title "The Age of my Father." The writer tells us how little joy or exuberance there was in the faith of his father. Whatever smelled of delight and pleasure was looked upon with a great deal of suspicion. It was also the age of my father. I know that time. Jesus was not that kind of a person. He changed water into wine so that the party could go on.

John says we saw then already something of his glory. Something beyond his humanity. True of course, but there is also something else to see: Jesus who wanted the party, the wedding to go on.

The other thing that struck me is the abundance of the miracle. Six jars of about one hundred litres. It's not like the 750 millilitre bottle that we bring to a party. We're talking about 600 litres here. I believe that too is a sign. His blessings are not doled out in minimal portions. The apostle Paul writes to the Ephesians about the riches of God's grace which he lavished on us. God's blessings do not come in small portions. His favours are not small stuff.

But let me tell lastly what speaks for me the loudest in this passage. The joy of the wedding is restored. Jesus restores joy. In some situations of life that seems even more impossible than this restoration of the wedding feast.

There is an incident in my pastoral career that I will never forget. The scene is in the waiting room next to the emergency unit in a hospital. The doctor had just come in with the sad news that the patient had died. The man suffered a sudden and fatal heart attack. I spent some time with the widow. There wasn't much I could say, but she said to me: "Now I am a widow and the joy is forever gone out of my life." I know I should not have said anything at all but in my eagerness to be of comfort I said: "There will be a time when joy will be restored in your life."

Years and years later I met this woman again. She smiled at me and she said that she had never forgotten what I said that night. She had clung to those few words and here she was. Smiling. Remarried and happy again.

At the end of that well known passage in Ecclesiastes three when the writer has spoken about the rhythm of life, a time to be born, a time to die. A time to mourn and a time to dance there is the end of the passage: "He has made everything beautiful in its time."

When the wine of life has run out Jesus restores the joy in his time. That I think is something that you can stick somewhere in your mind. It is unthinkable what tragedies can strike a human life. People cocooned in grief. There is sadness beyond comprehension. I know, and yet how often have I seen it, the restoration of joy. The return of laughter. The bounce back in the step.

How much time elapsed between Mary's asking and Jesus' acting? I don't know but I do know it is an anxious time. A time of depression. The time when the wine of life has run out. Imagine the family there at that wedding. What an embarrassment. What a tension. And then there is that glorious moment when the servants bring the new wine to the master of ceremonies. He is amazed. This is weird he says. Custom is to serve the good stuff first and after the guests are half way buzzed you bring out the cheap wine, but you have saved the best till now.

The time between Mary asking and Jesus acting could not have been that long, although we know that these parties could and would go on for days on end. But there must have been at least some time of waiting for Mary to see whether Jesus would act. What a difficult time that is. The time of waiting when it seems that your prayers bounce off against the heavens.

The Bible's example of one who gave up on the waiting is Abraham. He did not want to be on the waiting list any longer. There must be millions of people walking around with hopes blown away like tumble weed. With disillusioned lives. Waiting. It is the hardest thing to do. Wait. The ache of longing is painful.

Yet the preacher who in the Book of Ecclesiastes so clearly sets down the rhythm of the current of life: time to be born time to die. He concludes: "He has made everything beautiful in its time." Sometimes his time is beyond our time but than for sure he will wipe away the tears. In the end the darkness will give birth to light.

CHAPTER SIXTEEN
WORRY, THE CONSTANT COMPANION

It is about noon. The rain has stopped. I am in my own home. Even though the home consists of only two rooms, it is my home. I make valiant efforts to install the hearth which we bought second-hand some weeks ago. To my surprise I succeed in getting the thing in place. We have already some little bags of coal and soon there is a warm glow in the room.

Martha has emptied her wallet and found some money. Enough for the evening meal. I am totally, completely, absolutely dead broke. My last penny went to pay the wedding expenses. Including the limousines. I worry about money. It will be some weeks before I get another one of those envelopes in which they deposit your salary, minuscule as it is.

I have sold my motorcycle, but the fellow who bought it hasn't paid me yet. On my way home from Indonesia I was promised that the Dutch Department of Defense would pay for my education. I did enrol in a fairly expensive evening school. No money of the government has been forthcoming. Inquiries at the Department of Defense show that there is no money available. We are stuck with the monthly tuition bill.

I worry. Worry is a rodent that gnaws away at your peace. It is a poison that settles in your brain and intervenes with your normal thought processes. It is a dark prison cell where light cannot penetrate. I think about money all the time. Figures dance around in my thoughts like dervish dancers at a religious festival: rent, tuition, food, books, insurance and miscellaneous.

I share my worry about money with Martha. She is optimistic, and she also has that wonderful ability to really handle money very effectively. She thinks positively. And somehow she has managed to cook up this wonderful meal: sauerkraut with bacon. It is our first meal together.

I propose that we shall ever celebrate our anniversary with the same meal. Sometime during the evening my mother brings us the money that was owing to us from the sale of my motorcycle. It will last us for some time. "See," Martha says, "you worry too much." Yes I do. I know it. Yet the worry keeps me awake at night. I have anxiety dreams. I am too late for all kinds of departures. I miss books, and sometimes when I wake up I still grab for my rifle.

I am still not totally civilian. Army buddies keep visiting me, and a large part of my being is still foreign to this non-military life. One of the guys of my platoon has signed on for service in Korea. I know for sure that I will not join him. On the other hand I worry whether I will ever fit in to this polite, bourgeois environment in which I find myself.

Worry cleaves to me like a leech. It is like an unwelcome stranger that has come to stay and will not leave. Or will it?

JOSHUA 5: 12

Traditionally history has been divided into three periods: ancient, mediaeval and modern. Yet historians agree that we live in an entirely new epoch. A totally different era has begun. We don't know exactly when his new period started. Some say that the precise point in time when everything changed was when the Titanic was launched. Others argue that it was when the in the Nevada desert the first atomic explosion took place. And again different opinions hold to the fact that everything changed when the first computer was booted up. People who will come after us will be able to pinpoint where and when exactly the change was introduced. History is always written by hindsight.

So we understand that the Joshua passage which we read, describes in the closing verses the start of a new period for the people of God. The manna stopped. For forty years the Israelites had relied on that manna for their daily food. Every morning it had been there for the picking. When on a long gone morning it had first appeared, the people had asked Moses: "What is it?" Moses had answered: "It is the bread which the Lord has given you to eat." During that long forty year journey through the desert there had been no worry about food to eat.

There had been worries, disappointments, pain, war and misery, but never had there been a lack of manna. Morning by morning they gathered it, and on the sixth day they gathered twice as much as on other days so that they would rest on the sabbath. Every day of the week there had been manna. They baked it, they fried it, they boiled it, and they complained about the monotony of their daily diet. But the manna had always been there as the expression of God's caring providence. It had been a secure, seemingly inexhaustible source of food. For forty years the manna had never failed.

But on that fateful morning when the people set foot in the promised land, the manna stopped. What a change! What a profound and radical shift. Imagine; forty years there had been manna every morning for the picking, and all of a sudden it ceased to be there.

In that event, loaded with significance as it is, God is saying something. What I hear is something that has become one of the basic lessons of life: there is no free lunch. What I hear God saying is: no more hand-outs. From now on you are on your own. Somehow the situation resembles that of a child moving out of the parental house. No more mother cooking breakfast, or father handing out a weekly allowance. You are on your own.

And well do we know it. We haven't stopped worrying about eating and drinking and clothing. We have become the providers. God delegated the task of providing to us and on the whole we here on the North American continent have done pretty well. We have provided well for ourselves. From the milk and honey that awaited the Israelites when they entered the promised land we have greatly expanded our consumption. Milk and honey are still with us, but boy have we ever added to those two. From milk and honey we have gone to an endless series of consumer products. All wrapped neatly in plastic, coated with paint or sprayed with some chemical. From milk and honey we have graduated to an endless list of needs and demands. From automobiles and personal computers to paperclips and velcro strips on our jackets. From hazelnuts to prime rib roast and from popcorn to Russian Caviar at $ 500 per five hundred gram. We certainly have added to the milk and honey shopping list of the people who entered the promised land.

But we did pay a price didn't we? We have become so involved in the task of providing that we hardly know how to stop anymore. We have to have garage sales to get rid of some of our stuff. We have become such busy providers that we hardly have time anymore to be still and know who God is, or who we are ourselves for that matter. We have become such plodders that we cannot afford the time to stop and smell a rose. We have become so involved, preoccupied and consumed by our task of providing that we made wars about who would possess what.

When we left the milk and honey stage we became worriers who suffered from ulcers and headaches and a whole list of other ailments because of our fear that we could not provide enough. Jesus knew that of course. He watched the people whose forbears had entered the land where he lived and who had blessed that land for its riches of milk and honey. He watched the people who lived there. He used them as examples in his parable lessons: "The ground of a certain man produced a good crop, he thought to himself what shall I do."

See a worrier: what shall I do? A worried provider. Don't you see a bit of yourself in him? What shall I do? Savings bonds, at so many percent interest, or shall we buy a new car. What shall I do? How much shall I invest in my pension fund? What shall I do? Pay now or pay later? Where shall I deposit my money?

What shall I do? The thought of that man is our thought. His question is our question. His worry is our worry. What shall I do? And Jesus knows us and he says with emphasis: "Do not worry." The Bible repeats that quite often. "Cast all your cares on God," Peter says. And Paul writes to the Philippians: "Do not be anxious about anything." It is one of the main themes of the New Testament. Do not worry.

But we do argue with the Bible. With God himself even. The Psalmists, Job, Abraham; the Bible is full with people who argued with God. We do that too. God, we say, life is not so easy anymore as it was in the time when your son Jesus walked the dusty roads of Palestine. We cannot live on milk and honey anymore. Here see my monthly budget: insurance, property taxes and Visa, and a new raincoat for my wife. And notice how expensive things have become. It is easy to say do not worry, but for us who live in this time worry is a way of life.

And Jesus in that well-known passage that records the Sermon on the Mount looked at all those people, and then he looked around and saw this bird flying up there. He felt the grass under his feet. And Jesus did not reach in any book for an illustration of what he wanted to teach. Look at that bird, he said, you don't see it sowing or reaping or storing away in barns or locking stuff in safety deposit boxes, That bird is not buying any blue chip stock. And have you ever noticed the beauty of those lilies over there? They don't send for catalogues from retailers. And feel once with your bare feet the grass that you sit on. You think that came out of nothing?

Jesus points to God the provider by way of the birds, the lilies and the grass. God the caretaker of what lives and grows. God who makes the sun to shine and the rain to fall. God in whom we live and move and have our being. God of care and compassion. God who handles humankind with the touch of a loving parent, and who loves his creatures, the earth included.

The Joshua passage shows that God gave us the declaration of independence. The manna stopped. You are on your own. And everyone who comes home tired after a day of hard work, everyone whose eyes hurt from staring at the computer screen, everyone who plows the field, everyone who teaches students knows and agrees: yes we are on our own. Yet everyone who knows the least little bit about God also knows that he has not withdrawn from our labour as if he were a business partner whose share in the enterprise was sold.

The Bible calls us co-workers with God. He works together with us.

That is what Jesus wants all worriers to know. To all people who are so stuck in their anxiety that they have lost sight of God's partnership in providing, Jesus says: he you there sweating blood over your balance sheet; you there figuring our how to make ends meet; you there putting on your spectacles to read all the fine print in your insurance policies; look once at that bird in your tree, the chrysanthemum in your window, and the grass that you have to mow in the summer. Look at them all. See behind all of that the miracle of creation. And especially see the Creator. Jesus teaches us that the Creator knows that our life needs more care than the life of birds and plants, and that God graciously gives all that care.

We re-discover in Jesus' words the God who cares for his creation, ourselves included. The God who, and it is one of the best known verses in the Bible John 3:16, the God who loved the kosmos, the world, his creation so much that he gave his one and only son to reconcile himself to it. In Jesus' words we see again that God did not withdraw from our work of providing on that fateful morning when the manna stopped.

We realize anew that we are only middle management at best. The mysteries of growth and life and death are in God's hand. Who of us by worrying can add a single hour to his or her life? In all of our often feverish business we still depend on the grace of God our Father.

There is one more thought that came to me when I considered Jesus' words in that part of the Sermon on the Mount. So often the words of our Lord speak in so many ways and at so many levels. When I visit the country where I came from I always spend some time in the Rijksmuseum in Amsterdam. And I always stand for a little while in front of that famous painting of Rembrandt 'The Nightwatch'. And every time I discover details that I had not seen before.

That is also my experience when I consider the words of Jesus. All of a sudden I saw how much and how deeply God loves the species of animals he created, how he loves the wonderful flowers of the field, and how perhaps he is smiling about that wondrous

110

capacity of grass to grow again after a long winter or a long period of draught when we thought it had all died. You know how brown the lawn can look after it hasn't rained for a couple of weeks. You look at it and you think I never have to mow that patch again. Yet one shower and there you go again pushing the old lawnmower. Don't you read in the words of Jesus that God amuses himself with that. "He clothes the grass of the field," Jesus says.

Our neighbourhood has been honoured many a summer with the presence of a pair of cardinals and several mourning doves. They put on quite a concert in the morning. I love to listen to that, but God does too. In those Sermon on the Mount words of Jesus I see something of God's love for, and his pleasure in all the things he created. Psalm 104 says that God created the sea as a playground for the leviathan, the whale.

If God so loves his creation, if God feeds the birds, clothes the grass, and colours the flowers then we must express our gratitude by tenderly taking care of what God created. Our thanksgiving must also be expressed by handling God's handiwork with care and love and prudence.

In our ever ongoing efforts to provide after the manna stopped, we have done great harm to God's creation. Every tree that dies from acid rain is really proof that we do not sufficiently care for what God loves so much. Every bird that dies a miserable death in oil soaked waters is an accusation to humankind corporately.

Let we then in conclusion see the direction we receive in Jesus' words. We have seen that God has not withdrawn from our efforts to provide. We have heard the invitation to trust in God's providing care, and we heard the call to care for the creation.

The words: "Seek first his kingdom and his righteousness," have reference to the way in which we deal not only with each other, but they have reference also to our way of dealing with the birds of the air, the grass f the field and the flowers in the meadows.

Printed in the United States
49490LVS00001B/34-84